Folk Art
FURNITURE

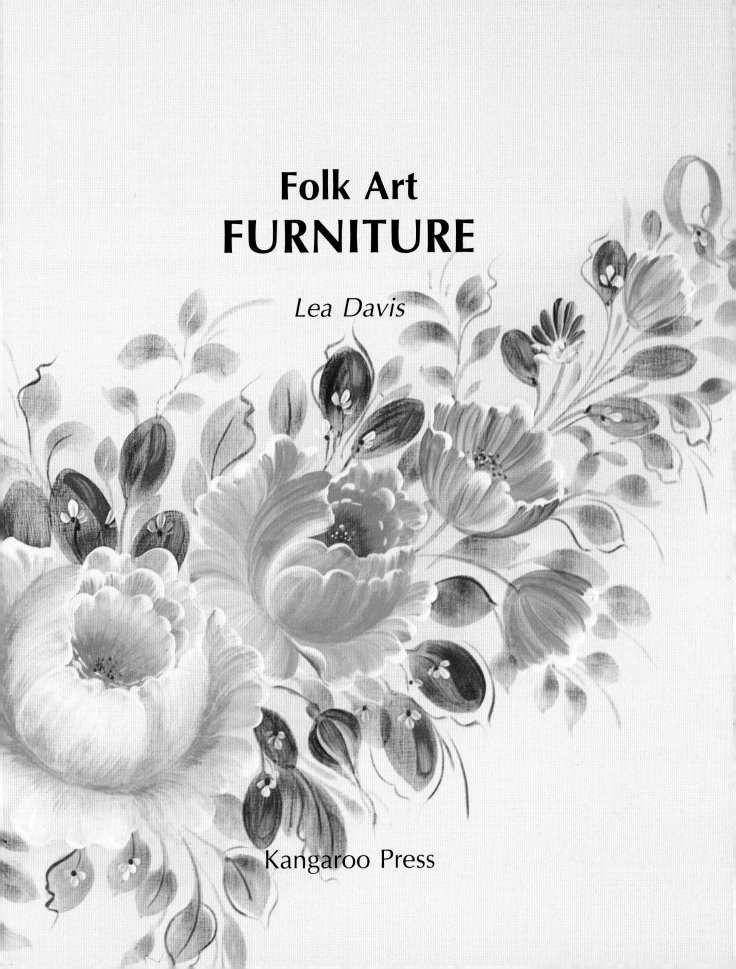

Folk Art
FURNITURE

Lea Davis

Kangaroo Press

Dedication

As always, for Colin

Acknowledgments

I find writing a book very difficult indeed. I know that as the final stages approach I am not an easy person to live with. So I would like to thank these members of my family, and my 'student family':

- My sons Mike and Tim, for bearing up under the strain
- My husband Philip—once again, thank you my darling
- My sister Susie and my brother-in-law Peter, who have encouraged and praised me all the way through
- My beautiful niece Casey and my nephew Scott for putting up with a lunatic for an aunty
- My mum and dad, who are always there when I need them, no matter for what, or when
- My students, who have faithfully given me the support and the time out when I needed it

I would also like to thank the following very special people who have given support, guidance and encouragement throughout the writing of the book, and who have given it freely and generously:

- Sue Schirmer, my special friend
- Andrina Jenkinson, whose help with the faux marbling was invaluable
- Joy Waters
- Karen Rowelle
- Sally Luck
- John Craddock
- Steven and Andrew Patterson from Matisse
- Barry Heard from Art Stretchers
- Bryce and Trish Dunkley for the wonderful photographs
- Carol, Graeme, Lauren, Brett and Ashlee Scott
- Frank Charlton, my father, who made all the cupboards, including the Schrank, and the screens on short notice, and with very vague instructions.
- And to Enid Hoessinger, thank you for your friendship and for all that you have taught me.

Please look out for DJ's Colour Conversion Chart, which will be available shortly. This chart enables you to find conversions to your favourite brand with over 2000 colours and mixes, with mixing ratios included. Brands covered are Matisse Flow Formula, Jo Sonja by Chroma Acrylics, Delta by Ceramcoat, Americana by DecoArt and Folkart by Plaid. This chart is a must for all folk artists, folk art teachers and studios.

© Lea Davis 1995

Reprinted 1998
First published in 1995 by Kangaroo Press
an imprint of Simon & Schuster Australia
20 Barcoo Street, East Roseville NSW 2069
Printed in Hong Kong through Colorcraft

ISBN 0 86417 718 6

Contents

INTRODUCTION

I have always loved the old, worn, time-affected pieces of furniture found in secondhand shops. I remember spending hard-earned dollars on a wonderful dresser when I first started college. My mother's exasperated looks didn't do anything to dispel the joy of owning my own 'antique' (only it wasn't an antique, just an ordinary old dresser). I loved just looking at it. I liked knowing it was there, in the corner of my room. It made me feel good. I used to wonder whose room it had graced before mine. There seemed to be so much history behind this piece (or so I imagined). I longed to be able to create something that would become a future antique, a piece that some other girl would run her hands over, and wonder as I did about the craftsperson who created it. An heirloom—made today, with tomorrow in mind, an article that future generations would enjoy and put in pride of place in their homes.

Here in this book are the results of those dreams (or at least some of them).

Lea Davis

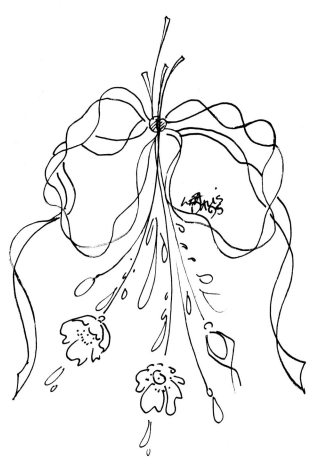

A WORD ABOUT THE PIECES

When I decided to write a book on larger items of furniture, I was hampered by the limited availability of pieces. Australia, as we all know, is very big and what is available in Melbourne may not be available in Darwin. I sincerely hope you will use the patterns to fit whatever pieces are available to you. I have given a few suggestions at the beginning of each section, but I know you will think of far more exciting adaptations than mine. Please experiment and be creative with your ideas. Reduce or enlarge the patterns for your use as you need. If you would like any help in adapting the patterns, or in fact in any way, please write to me at 51 Rosella Street, Murrumbeena, Victoria 3163.

BEFORE YOU BEGIN

Are you ready to begin thinking about your heirloom? It *will* be yours, even though you will use the patterns from this, or perhaps another, book. You are the one painting the piece and it will be your signature on the bottom. Remember—allow yourself weeks or even months to finish your piece, and never rush through the final stages. Your heirloom needs to be able to stand the test of time. To achieve that aim you will need to read the following section on paints and products carefully. Near enough is *not* good enough.

Please sign and date your piece. You may even consider listing other relevant snippets of information in an inconspicuous place, such as underneath, inside or on the bottom. For example, on the Schrank (page 62) I recorded the following on the back:

● Artist
● Furniture maker
● Type of wood
● Paints used
● Mediums used
● Varnishes (solvent/waterbased)
● Date started and date finished

I hope that in two hundred years time this information will make the restorer's job much easier.

BRUSHES, PAINTS AND MEDIUMS

Brushes

For most of the work in this book I have used a Rowney S40 size 3 sable hair brush. I also like the size 4, which I used to paint the pieces in *The Next Step in Folk Art*. As I explained then, sable hairs are naturally thicker in the middle of the hair and have more bounce and spring than synthetic fibres. By flattening out the hairs I am able to wash colour into a given area, and by thinning the paint and rolling the brush to a point I am able to paint very tiny lines. These brushes are my preference, but feel free to use either a flat brush or a liner brush if you would rather.

For the Rooster cupboard on page 45 I used a filbert brush (sometimes called a cat's tongue). This nifty little brush is like a flat brush with the corners cut off and is great for painting commas. It makes painting feathers much easier.

For varnishing I prefer to use a good quality 2.5 cm (1″) flat brush that I keep especially for varnishing. You get a wonderfully smooth finish with this brush.

A poly sponge brush is a cheap and effective means of basecoating large areas quickly. It's a little tricky to get into the corners though, so keep a brush handy. As soon as the brush becomes worn, discard it, as the sponge starts to break down and little bits end up stuck in the basecoating. I also use a 2.5 cm (1″) flat brush that I keep just for basecoating.

Paints

It is imperative that you use artist's quality paints and mediums for your work. They are heavily pigmented and are of heirloom quality. Do not mix different brands of paints.

Acrylic paint consists of a dry pigment, an acrylic polymer or copolymer emulsion and additives such as surfactants, preservatives, defoamers, glycols, solvents and thickeners. The additives are there to make the paint stable at freeze–thaw temperatures, to make it more workable, to make it stick to the surface and to achieve stability as it ages.

Acrylic paints, like all waterbased paints, need the addition of preservatives and fungicides to stop them from going mouldy. Different paint manufacturers may use a considerably different range of additives, some of which may not be compatible with other manufacturer's additives. Because the formulation of acrylic paints is so complex, it is not advisable to intermix different brands, especially when you are creating pieces that you want to last for centuries.

Mediums

Some of the mediums have uses other than those discussed below. I have only given instructions for the way I have used them throughout the book.

● *Jo Sonja's Tannin Blocking Sealer*
Use this product wherever the wood is knotty or dark coloured or even a little 'suspect'. This will prevent the pitch or tannin from coming through later and spoiling your painting. Apply a generous covering with a soft brush, brushing the medium well out around the knot.

● *Jo Sonja's Retarder and Antiquing Medium*
   DecoArt Americana's Brush 'n' Blend
   Matisse Drying Retarder
All three products retard the drying time of the paint, keeping the paint 'open' to allow longer working time. Use retarders sparingly, as they can keep the paint workable for too long, resulting in a sticky surface. They are compatible with water.

● *Clear Glazing Medium*
Mixed with paint, this product will reduce the opacity (opaqueness) of the paint, allowing transparent finishes to be obtained.

● *Matisse Faux Finish and Marbling Gel*
This product keeps the colours from mixing together during the faux marbling process.
DecoArt's Brush 'n' Blend Extender + Control Medium can also be used for faux marbling.

● *Matisse Pre-Antiquing Medium*
This formula creates a layer between the acrylic paint and the patina medium you will use when antiquing. This is especially important when the paint has been thinned with water, as in wash leaves, because the binder in the paint has been reduced. This means that the 'sticking' quality of the paint is now unstable and the paint could rub off during the antiquing process. By applying the Pre-Antiquing Medium you help solve this problem.

● *Patina Oil-Based Antiquing Medium*
This product is to be used with an oil paint, usually Burnt Umber (but consider also Burnt Sienna and Raw Umber).
1. Apply the Pre-Antiquing Medium and allow to dry for one hour.
2. Using a clean lint-free cotton cloth, apply the patina all over the surface.
3. Dab the cloth into a little oil paint and smear this over the surface of your work.
4. Wipe off the excess paint until you get the desired effect. If the antiquing is too dark, moisten a clean cotton square with patina and wipe over the surface to remove some of the colour.
5. Allow the antiquing to dry for 48 hours to a week before varnishing it.

Safety Warning
Wear disposable gloves when antiquing. When you have finished, wet the rags you having been using, place them in a plastic bag and throw them in the outside rubbish bin.

● *Matisse Final Varnish Gloss Finish* and *Final Varnish Matt Finish* (both mineral turps based)
I mix these two products together 1:1 in a separate container to arrive at a wonderful satin finish. The varnish is non-yellowing and quick to dry even though it is turps based. Normally I prefer to use water-based varnishes but this varnish has one very important feature—it's strippable. The varnish redissolves in mineral turpentine with very little effect on the painting underneath, so your heirloom can be cleaned and resurfaced safely.

If you would prefer a water-based varnish I suggest J.W. Etc's Right Step Satin Varnish, which can be applied over oil antiquing.

GLOSSARY OF BRUSH LOADING TECHNIQUES

This book assumes prior knowledge of the basic techniques of folk art painting as covered in *Introduction to Folk Art*. More advanced techniques are covered in *The Next Step in Folk Art*, and both these books should be referred to for full understanding of any terms not included here.

'To the surface/to the ceiling'

The instructions will sometimes ask you to hold the brush in a particular way or to apply the colour in a particular direction. This will usually be 'to the surface' or 'to the ceiling'. Do not get this confused with 'top' or 'bottom', which refers to the top or bottom of your piece (or the page if you are practising).

Wash

Thin the paint with water and test the depth of colour on a scrap of paper before you go onto your piece. After you have mixed the correct colour and consistency of paint, touch the loaded tip of the brush to a sheet of paper towel to help prevent puddles on your piece. Remember it is better to have a few light transparent washes rather than one heavy wash.

Wash leaves

There are two ways of painting in wash leaves. When the leaves are required to add bulk behind the design, chalk them onto the perimeter of the pattern, then pull them in freehand. Always keeping the flow of the pattern in mind, extend the wash leaves outside the perimeter a little.

The other way is to add the wash leaves when the main painting is finished. Pull the leaves in towards the design, wherever you feel there is a gap. Keep them flowing along with the feel of the design. I have omitted the wash leaves on the patterns because they make them too busy and hard to trace.

Sweep

After loading the brush in the main colour you are using, pull out a small amount of the second colour from the puddle of paint and sweep or wipe the hairs through this. You will not be loading the brush, but rather pushing the colour into the hairs. Do not aim for a great deal of paint. In this book you may be asked to sweep through three or even four colours. It is important to follow the order given in the instructions. For example, the instructions may say, 'sweep Antique Gold, sweep Yellow Light, sweep Titanium White'. You must sweep through the colours in that order, not randomly.

Fan-out centre

Load the brush in the main colour, say, Burnt Sienna mix. On the tip of the brush, on one side only, take on a small amount of, say, Antique Gold. On the *opposite* side, near the ferrule, take on a spot of black. Now lay the brush down in the pattern area with the black to the surface and fan out the strokes in an arch. Try to keep the ferrule in the one spot and pivot from there. If you feel that the paint is a little dry, especially if you are working on paper, touch the tip in a drop of water after you have loaded it with paint. This may take a little practice but persevere.

Sideload

After loading the brush in one colour, push the brush horizontally into the puddle of white paint (it doesn't necessarily have to be white) and pull it out towards you, lifting it towards your shoulder. It helps to have a strip of paint rather than a puddle. Don't drag the brush through the strip, push and lift.

Pull in

Using the sideloading technique pick up a load of white paint and lay it down along the pattern line. You will notice some flowers have very frilly skirts; in this case, when you are laying down the white you will have to use pressure to create an uneven edge. Apply pressure, then release, striving for an uneven and, in some areas, broken line. Work one area, or petal, at a time. Wipe the paint on some paper towel, and wipe or sweep the brush in the required flower colour, making sure the hairs on the brush flatten out. Push the flattened tip under the thick ridge of paint and pull the white down. Wipe off the excess paint, reload in the flower colour, and continue pulling the white down. Repeat for the rest of the petals. Look at the shape of the petal and the way it has been drawn and pull your strokes down accordingly. Very rarely, if ever, are the strokes straight. They always have some movement in them. While this is difficult to master in the beginning, it becomes easier with practice.

Here are a few points to remember:

1. Aim for a thick ridge of paint around the edge of the petals. Remember, it doesn't need to be even.
2. Wipe off the excess paint from the brush. Try to keep the brush out of the water unless you find it dragging across your work. Even then, touch the tip in a drop of water and go back to the palette and work it through.
3. Spread the hairs on the brush so that they fan out.

Dry-brushing

Used to give a hint of colour in a given area. Load the brush by sweeping the hairs through the paint. The paint brush should be flattened: if it isn't flatten it. Wipe any excess paint off lightly on some paper towel. Now, using the tips of the hairs, whisk the brush over the area to be covered. You should have the barest hint of colour, which you can reinforce if necessary by repeating what you have done.

Brush mixing

Rather than mixing the colours together on the palette with a palette knife, pick up the given colours on the brush. This gives a more casual feel to the work. Stroke the brush once or twice on the palette before making a stroke.

Criss-cross (or slip-slap)

Usually done with a large flat brush. Pick up one of the given colours on one side of the brush and the other colour on the other side. Imagine a series of Xs and apply the paint in this way, flipping the brush from side to side to use both colours. Keep overlapping the strokes all the time, but don't blend the two colours into one uniform colour. The aim is to give a soft muted base for the work on top. Sometimes the instructions will tell you to leave some texture in the background. To do this you will need to apply the paint rather thickly and lightly whisk over it with a coarse pastry brush or a cheap Chinese bristle brush such as those made under the brand name Eterna. Do this as the paint is drying.

If the instructions call for a softer blended look, as in the Cherub Screen on page 52, use a soft flat brush and blend the colours together without any texture. There should be a soft transition from, say, the outside edge into the middle, with no discernible line where the two meet.

Wet in wet

While the first layer of paint is still wet apply the next layer or section on top of it. Because the first layer is still wet there will be a slight blending of the two layers, usually resulting in a softer stroke.

11

This a bonus design not connected with the projects in the book.

Transferring a pattern

There are two ways of transferring a pattern. The first is to use transfer paper, available under brand names such as Cabin Craft and Saral. The other is to make your own transfer paper using ordinary blackboard chalk and tracing paper or greaseproof paper. Wherever you need to apply washes of colour it is safer to use the chalk method, because the marks left by commercial transfer paper may show through light washes. The marks can't be removed unless you take off all the wash and start again. If you trace on the pattern using the chalk method, the pattern lines disappear as soon as the water washes touch the chalk. This is ideal when working with transparent washes, but frustrating if you need to retain the pattern lines until the painting is finished. Thus there is a place for both methods.

To make your own transfer papers you will need a range of colours in ordinary blackboard chalk. There is a dustless brand available which is good. Trace your design onto the tracing paper or greaseproof paper. Turn the paper over and, using the appropriate colour chalk for your base colour (that is, one that will show up), rub the chalk over the back of the design. Rub the chalk into the paper with the pads of your fingers and shake off excess dust. Place the paper *chalk side down* where you want the design to appear and, using a stylus or pencil, trace around the design.

Distressing

This term can refer to the basecoat or to the wood itself. The aim of distressing is to damage the surface in some way so that the piece will look old and worn. There are a number of ways of achieving this, and I have dealt with a few in particular projects.

For information on Surface Preparation and Equipment, I suggest you refer to my previous books, *Introduction to Folk Art* and *The Next Step in Folk Art*, which deal with these areas in detail.

ROSES STEP BY STEP

First refresh your memory by revising the brush loading techniques listed in the Glossary on page 12, and revisiting the Roses Step by Step on pages 14 and 15 of *The Next Step in Folk Art*.

Palette (Matisse colours)
Antique Green mix—mix enough Mars Black into Yellow Light to make a mid-value green. Add a touch of Napthol Scarlet.
Burnt Sienna mix—mix enough Antique Green mix into Napthol Scarlet to tone the red down. The colour should still be discernible as red but on the brown side. (The tube Burnt Sienna is too dark.)
Antique Gold
Mars Black
Titanium White

Step 1 and 2   Place in the fan-out centre using Burnt Sienna mix, Antique Gold and Mars Black. Keep the original pattern in front of you as reference because you will paint over the lines.

Working quickly while the centre is still wet, sideload into Titanium White and push out the centre back petals. Wipe off the white paint on some paper towel, wipe in the Antique Gold then wipe in the Burnt Sienna mix and, with the gold to the surface, tuck the flattened-out hairs under the thick ridge of paint and pull the white down. You will only need small strokes.

Step 3   Let the black area and the centre dry before continuing. Sideload into Titanium White again and following the pattern lay down the white. Wipe the brush, sweep through Antique Gold, then Burnt Sienna mix, and pull the strokes down towards the outside edge. Try to curve the strokes rather than pull them straight down. Repeat the process on the opposite side, making sure to link up with the back petals on both sides. Use light pressure and keep up on the tip of the brush when starting off.

Step 4   Sideload into Titanium White and lay down the white on the top area of the middle petal. This petal needs to be lighter than the sides, so sweep through extra Titanium White if necessary. After laying down the white I usually pull the first stroke down one side, then the other, and lastly sweep through more white and pull the centre middle stroke through.

Step 5   Skirt petals: The technique is the same as before. Paint the two back petals on either side first. Curve your strokes and pull them towards you at all times, so you will have to turn the work around to complete the front petals.

Step 6   The turnback is painted separately after all the petals are finished. Load the brush in the Burnt Sienna mix, sideload in Titanium White and with the Burnt Sienna mix towards the bottom of the flower, link up the white to the existing petal, apply pressure, and lift off again to make a fine ending.

Tiny lines   For tiny lines in the centre, load the brush in Titanium White and flatten, then use the knife edge to pull tiny lines from the centre out. Turn the work upside down to make it easier.

Dots   Load the brush in Antique Gold then tip the end in Titanium White. Softly tap the dots in, using very light pressure. Don't overdo them.

Variations
1. *Multiple layers:* Start at the back of the rose as before in the step by step instructions (1). Add another row of petals inside the first (2). Now come to the front and connect up the second or inner row first, linking from front to back (3). Link up the second or front row (4), and paint as before. Finally the centre front petal is painted (5). Finish the skirt.

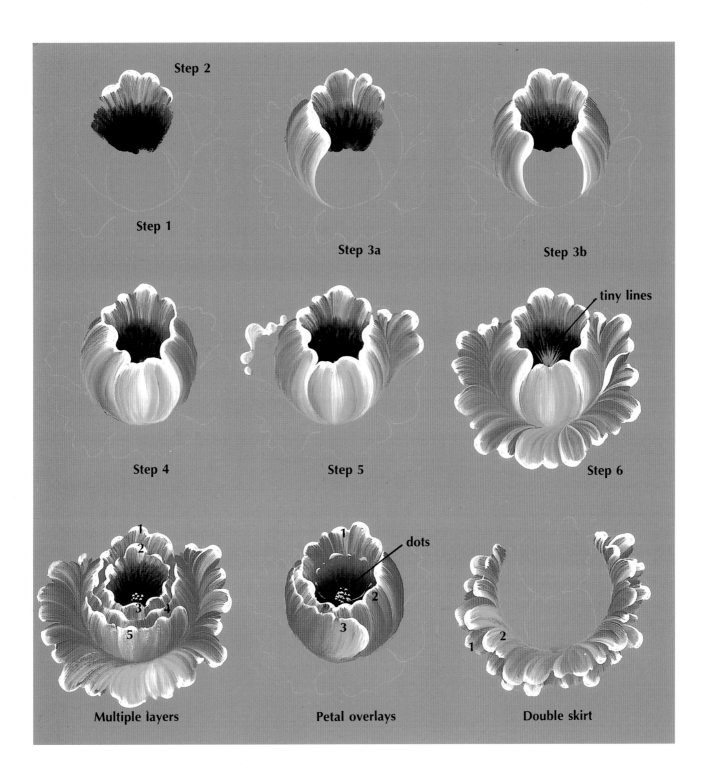

Step 2

Step 1

Step 3a

Step 3b

Step 4

Step 5

tiny lines

Step 6

Multiple layers

dots

Petal overlays

Double skirt

2. *Petal overlay:* Complete the petals up to step 4 of the step by step instructions (1,2). Keep the pattern out in front of you to refer to. Push out the white according to the pattern and pull down as before (3). Finish the skirt.

3. *Double skirt:* Complete one row of the skirt as in steps 5 and 6 of the step by step instructions. For the upper row push out the white in exactly the same way, but sit the edge inside the lower row. For contrast keep the underneath skirt fairly dark, or the top layer of petals won't be seen easily.

15

FAUX MARBLE STEP BY STEP

Read the instructions thoroughly to familiarise yourself with this technique before trying it. You will need to work quickly. The four panels show variations of the same basic technique. Try them all, then choose your favourite.

Palette
I have used Matisse paints and products. (Please note: B denotes a background colour available only in a jar, and T denotes tube colour. Matisse supplies Antique Blue in both jar and tube—they are *different colours*.)

Materials
Faux Finish and Marbling Gel (this keeps the colours from mixing together)
An old shaving brush or a blush brush
Plastic wrap
Assorted feathers
Mop brush

Panel 1:
Antique Blue background paint (B)
Pale Beige background paint (B)
Mix the above colours 1:1 to make a mix referred to as the 'Schrank colour' (it's used in the Schrank on page 62).
Antique Blue (T)
Antique White

1. Basecoat the background with Antique Blue (B).
2. Apply the Marbling Gel thickly and while wet apply the Schrank colour.
3. Pounce the shaving brush over the surface to remove the brushstrokes.
4. Place the plastic wrap over the surface and move it around gently with your fingers. Lift off and discard. Mix Antique Blue (T) with water. Drag a shaggy feather through the paint/water mix, and start pulling diagonal veins.
5. Gently whisk the mop brush over the entire surface, changing direction constantly. You will see how this sinks the vein lines into the surface and at the same time softens the plastic wrap background.
6. Repeat this step using watery Antique White.

7. Repeat with thicker paint, making certain to keep the veins very fine.
8. Occasionally have one vein line cutting diagonally across the main flow of veins to represent a fracture. Try to keep the effect subdued rather than too busy.

Panel 2:
Antique White + Pale Beige (B) mixed 1:1 (makes Cream)
Schrank mix from above
Antique Blue (T)
Antique White

1. Basecoat the background in the Cream mix.
2. Apply the Marbling Gel.
3. Paint on the Schrank mix.
4. Apply the plastic wrap.
5. Feather in soft veins in Antique Blue (T).
6. Feather in soft veins in Antique White.
7. Feather in thinner darker veins in thicker Antique Blue (T) + Antique White.

Panel 3:
Antique Blue (B)
Cream mix from above
Antique Blue (T)

1. Basecoat in Antique Blue (B).
2. Apply the Marbling Gel.
3. Brush on the Cream mix.
4. Apply the plastic wrap.
5. Feather in veins in Antique Blue.

Panel 4:
Antique Blue (B)
Cream mix
Antique Blue (T)
Antique White
N.B. This sample doesn't use any Marbling Gel.

1. Basecoat in Antique Blue (B).
2. Apply very watery Cream mix and then immediately apply the plastic wrap.

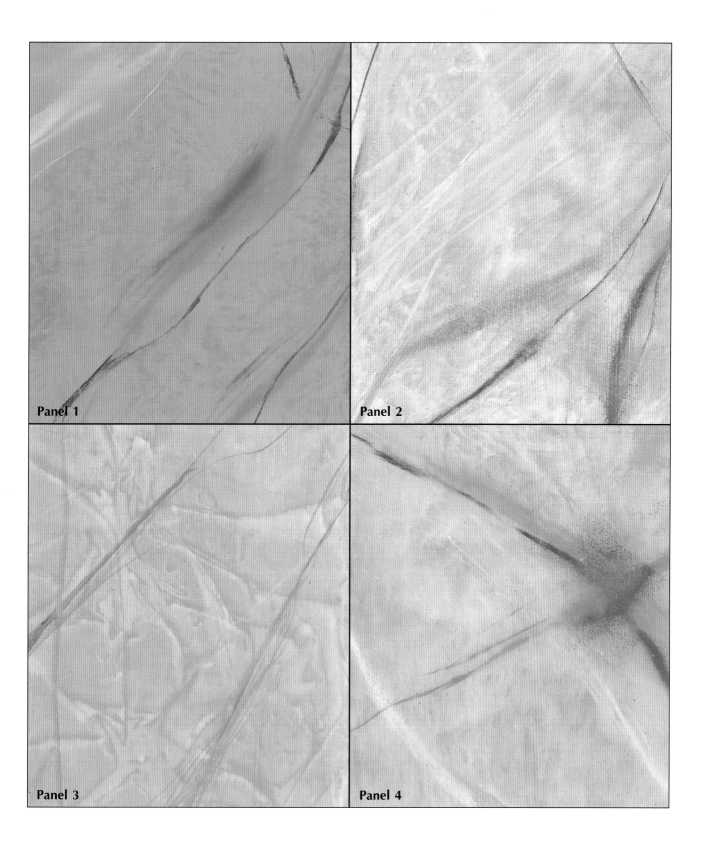

Panel 1

Panel 2

Panel 3

Panel 4

3. Dry, then feather in veins in Antique Blue (T).
4. Feather in more veins in Antique White.

You may like to try using a large sea sponge instead of plastic wrap. Apply the Marbling Gel as before, moisten the sea sponge, and pounce it in the watery colour of your choice. In the colours used above it would be either Cream mix or blue. Follow the same steps from there on.

eyes

teardrop

Teddy bear step by step instructions are on the following page

TEDDY BEAR STEP BY STEP

Follow the colour worksheet closely while reading these instructions. You may find the following hints helpful.

- I use ³⁄₈'' and ¹⁄₈'' deerfoot stipplers for this work. The brushes must be dry before starting the stippling. Deerfoot brushes are cut on an angle. If you turn the brush with the long edge to the surface you can use this side to tap into small areas, e.g. around the muzzle, under the chin.
- To prevent paint drying near the ferrule work a little Drying Retarder medium into the bristles before you begin painting. When loading the paint into the brush, pull the paint away from the puddle in a wiping motion to ensure you don't load the brush with excess paint.
- Wipe the brush on paper towel after you have put the colour into it.
- Do not wash the brush while in the middle of painting a teddy, rather, if absolutely necessary, wipe clean in Drying Retarder.
- Work on one area of the teddy at a time, first applying Drying Retarder with a flat brush. For example, start with half the head and one ear, then do the other half of the head. Try and work from the back to the front, so that anything that is behind and underneath will be painted first and the next area will sit slightly over. This will create a furry look.
- Aim for a semi-opaque look rather than solid colour. I love the wood grain showing through—it looks as though the painting is sinking into the wood.
- You will be working with three or more values of colour—a shade, a middle value and a highlight colour or colours. Keep the shade and highlight colours separated by the middle value.
- Use the chalk method for transferring the pattern. With other types of transfer paper you run the risk of the pattern lines showing through the painting. Trace only the lines that are necessary, using a light touch so as not to dent the wood surface.

Palette (Matisse colours)
Shade: Mix Burnt Umber + Burnt Sienna
Middle value: Yellow Oxide
Highlight: Turner's Yellow + Antique White

1. Trace the pattern using the chalk method.
2. Apply Drying Retarder to the head area. Try to keep inside the pattern lines or they will disappear when the Drying Retarder touches them. Wipe the brush in Yellow Oxide, wipe lightly on the paper towel and using a pouncing motion apply the colour to the ear.
3. Move down onto the face and stipple around the muzzle. Wipe in more Yellow Oxide if necessary, wiping off on the paper towel as before.
4. Wipe the brush on the paper towel and wipe in the shade mix. Wipe lightly on the paper towel.
5. Apply the shade mix in the ear, on the face around the bandage and around the muzzle (nose), and the eye sockets. Wipe the brush.
6. Now go back to the ear and soften where the two colours meet. Do the same wherever the two colours meet. If you feel the yellow is becoming brown, wipe the brush, wipe in the Yellow Oxide again and go back and blend the colours. At no time do we want a hard line of shade colour.
7. Wipe the brush and load back in the Yellow Oxide. Pounce in the muzzle, keeping to the pattern lines.
8. Wipe the brush, wipe in the shade colour and place a soft shade at the bottom of the muzzle behind the teddy's hand. Blend the colours together.
9. Wipe the brush, wipe in the highlight colour and pounce the highlight softly on the top of the muzzle and on the top of the ear.
10. Apply Drying Retarder to the arm holding the baby teddy.
11. Apply Yellow Oxide to the arm, and shade as before. Blend.
12. Wipe the brush, wipe in the highlight colour and apply this to the outside edge of his arm. Don't go up

underneath his chin or around his hand.

13. Retard the tummy area and apply the Yellow Oxide.

14. Wipe the brush, wipe in the shade mix and shade under his arm and along under his chin. Wipe the brush and blend softly.

15. Wipe the brush, wipe in the highlight mix and starting in the middle of the tummy apply the highlight, softly pouncing around in a circle. Don't go too far out. Wipe the brush and blend softly.

16. Retard the other arm. Apply the Yellow Oxide, wipe the brush, wipe in the shade mix and apply this to the elbow. Blend softly. Highlight the paw near the muzzle.

17. Retard both legs. Apply the Yellow Oxide, wipe the brush, wipe in the shade mix and shade underneath his tummy at the top of his legs and also on the bottom of his feet.

18. Wipe the brush, wipe in the highlight mix and highlight across the top of his foot.

19. Block in the bandage with Antique White. You will need two coats. Mix Antique White + a touch of Mars Black to make grey and wash in the shade lines on the bandage.

20. The eyes are painted in Mars Black. Use small strokes and feather them out to represent eyelashes. Block in the nose with Mars Black. See the detail beside the teddy.

21. Add an Antique White highlight to the eye. Keep it soft. Take a little Mars Black and softly pat over it to sink it back. Add an Antique White highlight to the tip of the nose. You may like to add some very soft Antique White eyelashes as well. I have dry-brushed some Antique White underneath the eyebrows before painting them in Mars Black.

22. The teardrop: Paint the hook in Antique White. Keep it very fine and make sure it conforms in shape to the surface it rests on. Shade underneath and a little way up the side with the shade mix. Wash Antique White inside the hook, keeping the drop shape. This is the bright side of the drop so it should be facing the light source if there is one. Make tiny reflected light dots on the opposite side of the Antique White wash (this would be opposite the light source).

23. Finally, using thinned shade colour, add fine broken lines around the edges of the teddy. Keep them loose and have stray strokes sticking out at odd angles. This needs a little practice.

24. Baby teddy: Pounce in in Turner's Yellow, shade with Burnt Sienna and highlight with Turner's Yellow + Antique White. Add Mars Black eyes, nose and linework.

Practice the teddy bear technique a few times before going on to your wood piece.

Teddy bear hospital trunk

Patterns on pages 72–77

This beautiful wooden trunk belongs to Sue Schirmer, a very special friend. I hope you enjoy painting the teddies—they are so easy. They lend themselves to a natural wood-grain more than to a painted background. You don't have to paint them all, try just two or three first.

This trunk is 76 cm long by 35 cm high by 34 cm deep (30″ × 14″ × 13½″).

Palette (Matisse colours)
Napthol Scarlet
Yellow Oxide
Antique White
Burnt Sienna
Turner's Yellow
Antique Blue
Raw Sienna
Vermilion
Mars Black
Burnt Umber
Titanium White
Ash Pink

Please refer to the step by step instructions on pages 21–22 for painting teddies. I have given the special instructions for each individual teddy here but have not repeated the general 'how to paint' information.

Good bear teddy

Mixes
1. *Medium value:* Napthol Scarlet + Raw Sienna 1:1
2. *Highlight:* Yellow Oxide + Vermilion + Antique White 2:1:1
3. *Brighter highlight:* Equal parts Antique White + Raw Sienna + Yellow Oxide.

Shade Burnt Sienna. For the darker areas use Burnt Sienna + Burnt Umber.

Painting sequence Apply mix 1 (medium value), then shade with Burnt Sienna and, if needed, Burnt Umber.

Highlight with mix 2, then reinforce with mix 3 in a smaller area. Use the highlights sparingly as this teddy is quite dark.

Nose Mars Black, then brush a little Burnt Sienna over the highlight area. Add Antique White and blend slightly.

Mouth Shade the mouth with Burnt Umber and highlight with mix 3.

Eyes Shade behind the eye-socket with Burnt Umber and while this is still wet highlight inside the area with mix 2. Fan out Mars Black from the eye socket to represent eyelashes. Block in the iris with a mix of Burnt Umber + Mars Black and highlight the iris with Antique White. Add a few random highlights around the eyes with mix 3.

Bandage Block in with Antique White + a touch of Burnt Sienna. The knot is Titanium White outlined in a mix of Antique White + Mars Black (medium grey).

Badge Base in Antique White and outline in mix 3. Write GOOD BEAR in Mars Black.

Linework The linework around the teddy is a watery mix of Mars Black + Burnt Umber.

Ice pack teddy

Mixes
  1. *Medium value:* Turner's Yellow + Ash Pink 1:1
  2. *Shade:* Burnt Sienna + Turner's Yellow 2:1
  3. *Highlight:* Turner's Yellow + Antique White 1:4
Add extra highlights with Antique White where needed.

Eyes and eyelashes Mars Black. Pupil is Burnt Sienna with an Antique White highlight. Linework and eyebrows are mix 2 + Burnt Umber.

Nose Mars Black with a highlight of Antique White + a touch of Burnt Sienna.

Ice pack Start with 2 or 3 coats of Antique White. Mix Antique White + a touch of Mars Black and place in the creases. Wash along one edge to softly fade out. Add Titanium White highlights along the sharp edge of the crease (the side you haven't shaded).

Teardrop teddy

The instructions for this teddy appear in full on page 21.

Pillow teddy (he has a fever)

Pillow Block in with Antique White. You will need 2 or 3 coats. Apply the pattern to get the line direction. Wash Antique Blue down either end to shade. Thin this down and place in the lines.

Mixes
1. *Medium value:* Burnt Sienna + Yellow Oxide 1:1
2. *Shade:* Burnt Sienna
3. *Highlight:* Turner's Yellow, then additional highlights of Turner's Yellow + Antique White

Blush on the cheeks is Napthol Scarlet + Antique White. Eyelashes, mouth and nose are Mars Black. Highlight the nose, above the eyebrows, above the eyelashes and around the mouth with Antique White.

Linework is a mix of Burnt Sienna + Burnt Umber.

When the teddy is finished wash Antique Blue around his head where it rests on the pillow.

Sore paw teddy (on the lid)

This little fellow is painted in the same colours as the teardrop teddy in the step by step instructions on pages 21–22.

Beary good bear (on the lid)

This teddy is painted in the same colours as the good bear teddy on page 23. His eyepatch is Mars Black with Antique White highlights. Add a Napthol Scarlet heart and paint the words BEARY GOOD on his badge.

Finishing

Let the trunk dry completely. Then moisten the area around the bears' feet with water. Using a large flat brush casually apply Burnt Sienna around their feet and down to the edge of the trunk. Softly fade it out into the background.

Around the lid and on the lid drop I have painted a 3 cm (1¼″) band of Antique Blue.

Varnish with your favourite varnish to finish.

Floral clock

Pattern on page 80

The clock face is 30 cm (12″) in diameter.

Palette (Jo Sonja colours)
Antique Green
Napthol Red Light
Titanium White
Ultramarine Blue
Yellow Light
Indian Red Oxide
Rich Gold
Carbon Black
Antique Gold
Burnt Umber
Warm White
Raw Sienna
Smoked Pearl
DecoArt American Weathered Wood
Burnt Umber oil paint

You will need a size 10 or 12 flat brush and a size 8 flat brush for this project. A coarse 2.5 cm (1″) pastry bristle brush or a stiff hog's-hair brush is also required.

Paint the sides and back of the clock with two coats of Indian Red Oxide. Sand lightly. Using the dry-brush method randomly brush Rich Gold over the back and sides. Basecoat the front with two coats of Smoked Pearl. Trace the outer circles onto the face of the clock—this is the area that will have the washes of colour on it. Paint between the circles with one even coat of Indian Red Oxide and when dry apply Weathered Wood over the Indian Red Oxide. Dry.

Into separate containers squeeze Smoked Pearl and Warm White. Using the 10 or 12 flat brush pick up Smoked Pearl on one side of the bristles and Warm White on the other. You will have a fair amount of paint on the brush. Starting at the top of the clock surround, place the brush onto the surface (it doesn't matter which colour is first) and flip it from one side to the other, picking up more paint as needed. Try and bring texture into the surface without having big lumps of paint. Using the 2.5 cm (1″) bristle brush gently whisk over any uneven areas, keeping the brush strokes moving in all directions. Paint the lower part of the surround the same way. Now swap to the size 8 brush for the face of the clock and apply the paint in the same way. Apply the paint to the Indian Red Oxide area in the same way also but *don't* overbrush this area or it will not crackle. (You should be able to see the crackles almost straight

away.) Dry, and apply the patterns to the top and bottom of the clock surrounds.

Leaves Mix Antique Green with a little Carbon Black and base in all the large solid leaves. A few have Antique Gold highlights on them where they overlap. Paint veins on the leaves using Antique Gold on the knife edge of your brush. For the stems, load the brush in the Antique Green + Carbon Black mix and sweep through Antique Gold. Hold the brush on the knife edge.

Roses If necessary, refer to *The Next Step in Folk Art*, pages 14 and 15, for step by step instructions for the left-hand rose. (The completed rose, using the colours for this project, is shown on the opposite page.) The rose on the right is shown on page 15 of this book.

Use the following colours for both roses: Mix Napthol Red Light + Carbon Black until you arrive at a burgundy colour. You will need more red than black. To some of this mix add a little Titanium White so that you now have two values of burgundy. Place in the fan-out centre using the dark burgundy mix, Antique Gold and Carbon Black. Push out the edge in Titanium White. Wipe the brush, sweep through the dark burgundy mix and pull the strokes down towards the centre. Repeat for all the petals, keeping the petals at the front lighter by sweeping in the lighter mix as you move towards the front of the flower.

Cup flower Mix Napthol Red Light + Ultramarine Blue + Burnt Umber to make a soft mauve. Push out the edges of the petals with Titanium White, wipe the brush, sweep through the mauve mix and pull the white down. Remember to start at the back and work one petal at a time. The dots in the centre are Antique Gold, then Antique Gold + Yellow Light. The small pink cup flowers are painted with a mix of Napthol Red Light + Carbon Black + Titanium White (the rose mix).

Wash leaves Using the leaf mix add wash leaves randomly over the design area. Use the dark rose mix (Napthol Red Light + Carbon Black) to add wash leaves also.

Circular surround Carefully apply the divisions to the crackled area following the pattern. Apply the washes over the page in sequence, remembering to thin the paint with water:

Leave one plain
1. Napthol Red Light + Carbon Black + Titanium White (rose mix)
2. Antique Green + Carbon Black (leaf mix)
3. Napthol Red Light + Burnt Umber + Ultramarine Blue + Titanium White (cup flower mix)

Repeat the colours around the circle. Paint a thin line on the inner edge of the divisions with mix 3.

Clock face   The line which the numbers sit against is mix 2. Add tiny wash leaves around this line with the same mix. Trace on the numerals and the pattern for the clock face flowers. Paint the numerals with the dark burgundy rose mix, using a liner brush. The flowers are painted using the same colours as those on the top of the clock. Review your work, adding wash leaves as required.

When dry, antique the whole surface with Burnt Umber oil paint. When the antiquing is dry use 000 or 0000 steel wool to lightly buff the surface. The steel wool will take the antiquing off the raised parts of the paint, adding more highlights.
    Varnish with your favourite varnish.

My friend Sue Schirmer from VADA in Melbourne painted the hands of the clock for me. She felt the original gold hands looked wrong and went over them with Indian Red Oxide.

Blue stool

Pattern on page 82

Crocus

Morning
glories

Honesty

Fuchsia

Large
daisies

Aster

Daisies

Cup flowers

Field
roses

This stool was a 'find' my husband made at a clearing sale in Bendigo, Victoria. My father sanded it down and I went to work on it. The wood was fairly rough and splintery but that only added to the distressed look I was trying to get.

The floral wreath would look marvellous also on a tray or box lid, as a table centrepiece, clock face or doily cover, or on a toilet lid.

Palette (Jo Sonja colours)
French Blue
Warm White
Titanium White
Paynes Grey
Moss Green
Storm Blue
Napthol Red Light
Antique Gold
Diox Purple
Fawn
Napthol Crimson
Burgundy
Cadmium Yellow Mid
Carbon Black
Clear Glazing Medium
Matisse Burgundy

This project is worked on raw wood so any piece already varnished must be sanded down first. Mix French Blue and Clear Glazing Medium 2:1 and basecoat the piece with this. Allow to dry for a few hours, but not overnight. Now mix Warm White with enough Clear Glazing Medium to make a transparent glaze. The white should look like a bloom on the blue background, but not cover it. If it isn't heavy enough add more paint, if too dark add more Glazing Medium. Working one section at a time so you can control the drying time of the paint, apply the Warm White mix over the French Blue basecoat and wipe it off again after a few minutes. You should aim to rub some areas back to the raw wood. Coat again with the Warm White mix if necessary. When dry, sand lightly.

Centre the design on your piece and trace a circle through the middle of the design as a guide, without applying the pattern at this point. Add enough water to some Paynes Grey to paint in the wash leaves. Keep the flow of the circle as you move around it. Allow to dry, and apply the pattern.

Leaves   Block in the leaves with Storm Blue. Where they overlap, highlight the top leaf with a sideload of Antique Gold. Add veins with Storm Blue swept with Antique Gold. On the two leaves on the pattern marked with a P use the pull-in technique, laying Antique Gold around the edge and pulling-in with Storm Blue.

Pansies   Please refer to the colour step by step for the Pansies Bedhead on page 72. The pansies are numbered on the pattern to correspond to these three colourways:
1. Mix Burgundy + Moss Green + Warm White to make a soft pink, and block in the shape. Wash a Warm White patch on the back petals, and wash around the edges with Burgundy. Tiny lines on the front petal are Warm White.
2. Block in the shape with Diox Purple. The back four petals are washed around the edges with Cadmium Yellow Mid. The front petal has Warm White washed around the edge. Tiny lines on the front petal are Warm White.
3. Block in the shape with Cadmium Yellow Mid. Wash around the edges with Matisse Burgundy. Tiny lines on the front petal are Matisse Burgundy.

All three pansies have a Cadmium Yellow Mid dot in the centre and Warm White dribbled around the edges.

Morning glories   There are three of these. They are numbered on the pattern to correspond to the following:
1. Mix Napthol Red Light + Warm White + Carbon Black (just a touch) to get a soft burgundy pink. Push out the edge in Titanium White and pull down the colour in the pink mix.
2. Push out the edge in Antique Gold, and pull down the colour with Warm White.
3. The back petals are painted first. Push out the edge with Diox Purple and pull down the colour with Titanium White. Link up the front petals with the back, again with Diox Purple. Pull the colour down with Titanium White.

All calyxes are Storm Blue swept through Antique Gold for the two outside parts or sepals, then swept through a small amount of Titanium White for the middle one.

Field roses   There are three of these, numbered on the pattern to correspond to the following:
1. Mix Napthol Red Light + Warm White + a touch of Carbon Black to make a burgundy pink (the same mix used for one of the morning glories). Push out the edge in Titanium White and pull the colour down with the pink mix.
2 and 3.   Use the same mix as above, adding a little more Napthol Red Light to make a sweeter pink. Push out the edge with Titanium White, and pull down with the sweeter pink mix.

All flipbacks are painted with the white held to the inside of the petal and the darker colour to the outside.

To paint the centres, dab Antique Gold in the centre in an oval shape. Touch into a little of the darker colour and dab just underneath the first oval. Finally dab in

Titanium White inside the first Antique Gold oval. Add tiny dots of Titanium White, then Antique Gold.

Crocus Mix Diox Purple with a little Fawn. Load the brush in this mix, sweep through Antique Gold, hold the gold to the surface and place in the centre middle back stroke. Sweep through a little more Antique Gold and paint in the rest of the petals. Keep the two outside ones dark because they have flipbacks on them. Add the flipbacks now with Titanium White, keeping them small. Load the brush in the purple mix, sweep Antique Gold then sweep Titanium White. With the white held to the surface pull the middle strokes through. You will need two strokes to fill this in. Mix Cadmium Yellow Mid + Matisse Burgundy to make orange and place in the stamens. Place tiny Cadmium Yellow Mid strokes on the tip of these.

Cup flowers Push out the edge with Matisse Burgundy and pull the colour down with Cadmium Yellow Mid. Add the flipback last.

Fuchsia Load the brush in Titanium White and tip the end in Diox Purple. Place two strokes side by side for the petals. For the calyx, mix Napthol Crimson + a touch of Carbon Black. Load the brush in this, sweep through Antique Gold, hold the gold to the surface and paint one small blob then a bigger one underneath. Paint two S strokes for the outside sepals and fill in the middle one. When dry, dry-brush on a little Warm White.

Aster Mix Napthol Red Light + Warm White + a touch of Carbon Black to make the burgundy mix. Place in the petals underneath the flower (see colour work-up). Sweep through Titanium White and place in the next lot of petals. Sweep through Titanium White again and lastly place in the top petals. Keep the lightest petals to the centre front. Dry-brush Titanium White onto the tips of a few bottom front petals. For the centre, load the brush in Antique Gold then touch the tip in the burgundy mix and tap in an oval. Pick up a little Titanium White on the tip and place that inside the oval. Load the brush in the burgundy mix, sweep through Titanium White and place in tiny petals around the centre, holding the white to the outside for each stroke. The aster bud is painted the same way. Paint the calyx in the leaf mix swept through Antique Gold. Sweep through Titanium White for the centre front sepal.

Large pink daisies Push out the edge in Titanium White, then pull down the edge with the burgundy mix. Dab in a centre of Antique Gold then add a shadow on the bottom edge with the burgundy mix. Add dots of both Antique Gold and Antique Gold + Titanium White.

Small daisies Load the brush in Titanium White and using the knife edge pull in the back petals. Add small dabs of white across the front to represent turned up petals. For the centre, load the brush in Antique Gold and sideload in Titanium White, push the white to the top of the centre and lift off.

Honesty Two knife strokes of Titanium White make one petal. Keep them light. Add a tiny dot of Storm Blue in the centre.

Snowdrops Place in the stems with the leaf mix. The petals are S strokes of Titanium White.

Dead rose calyx Load the brush in the leaf mix, sweep through Antique Gold and place in the two back sepals. Sweep through Titanium White and place in the other two. Tiny lines of leaf mix for the stamens with Antique Gold, then Antique Gold + Titanium White dots on the ends.

Filler flowers and strokes Titanium White flowers with a dot of Matisse Burgundy then a smaller dot on top of Cadmium Yellow Mid. Filler strokes are leaf mix for the stems, then tiny Titanium White dots along one side.

I chose not to antique this piece but you may like to. If you do, use Burnt Umber oil paint and antique lightly. Varnish in either case.

Butler's tray

Pattern on page 84

This butler's tray is a great idea. The large tray lifts off and the legs fold up for storage. The tray measures 61 cm by 48 cm (24″ × 19″). I wanted the design to look like strewn flowers—as if a bouquet of flowers had been thrown onto the tray. I hope you like it. Other places to use this design might include sofa or coffee tables, dining tables and bedside tables.

Palette (DecoArt Americana colours)
Blue Violet
Antique Gold Deep
Snow White
Yellow Light
Brilliant Red
Ebony Black

Glorious Gold
Jo Sonja's Indian Red Oxide
Clear Glazing Medium

Basecoat the tray and legs with two or three coats of Indian Red Oxide. Apply the pattern for the main leaves and the rosebuds, the peonies, and the pink and yellow blossoms. Omit the fluffy daisies because the pattern for these must be transferred using the chalk method.

Leaves   There are heaps of them! The ones in the centre of interest have the most work on them. The wash leaves are there just to add interest and to fill in the background area. The colour for the leaves is a 2: 1:1 mix of Yellow Oxide + Ebony Black + Brilliant Red,

which is a deep, dark red-brown. When squeezing out the colours make the puddles uniform or the colour will be wrong. A chocolate chip is a good size to approximate.

Working one leaf at a time, base in the shape quickly. Rough edges are fine at this stage. Wipe the brush in Yellow Light and, starting near the centre vein and working towards the tip, place comma strokes one after the other, gently curving them to the outside edge. Do not reload the brush halfway through a side or the colour will be different. Repeat for the other side. Paint all the large leaves this way. The large leaf in the middle of the pattern with a W on it is painted the same way except that after sweeping through Yellow Light, sweep also through a small amount of Snow White; place in the strokes as before. This leaf must sit over the others because it is lighter.

I would add some wash leaves now, although they could be added at any stage. Make a burgundy colour by mixing Brilliant Red + Ebony Black + a small amount of Yellow Light. Thin this mix with water and randomly scatter them in as in the photograph on page 36.

Tulip Make a Raw Sienna colour by mixing Yellow Light + a small amount of Brilliant Red + a touch of Ebony Black. Follow the numbers on the pattern for petal painting order. Push out the edges in Snow White. Wipe the brush in the yellow mix, flattening out the hairs, and pull down the white. Curve your strokes. Paint petal 3 then place in the flipbacks. For the front petal, add a touch of Brilliant Red to the yellow mix to brighten it, then push out the edge again in Snow White. Wipe the brush, wipe in the new yellow mix and pull the white down. Sweep through extra white for the centre stroke to make that area whiter and appear to move forward. Add a touch of Ebony Black to the yellow mix and pull tiny lines up from the bottom of the tulip.

Peonies These two large ruffled flowers are both painted in the same way, but the step by step refers to the pink one, the more difficult of the two.

Paint the white peony as numbered on the pattern, starting with Yellow Light + a small amount of Brilliant Red + a touch of Ebony Black. This is the same mix

used in the tulip. Use this in the darker areas of the flower, adding more white as you move towards the front. Push out the edge in Snow White as before. For the centre mix Brilliant Red + Ebony Black to make a burgundy colour and dabble this in before the front petals are painted. While wet pick up Yellow Light and Snow White and place in the stamens. Add a few comma strokes of Brilliant Red for stamens. Add tiny strokes on the top of some of the stamens with the burgundy mix sideloaded with Snow White. Place these across the top of the stroke.

Pink peony Mix Brilliant Red + Ebony Black to make a burgundy colour. To half of this mix add enough Snow White to make a soft middle-value pink. Following the number sequence on the pattern, and using the dark half of the mix, paint in the petals numbered 1 through 6, pushing out the edge in Snow White.

For petal 7, increase the white by sweeping through Snow White after sweeping through the dark mix. Hold the white to the surface, and pull the white down.

For petals 8, 9, 10 and 11 push out the edge in Snow

White and sweep through the lighter mix to pull the white down.

Place in the centre now, before painting petal 12. Load the brush in Antique Gold Deep and touch the tip in Brilliant Red. Tap around the centre in an oval. On the dirty brush pick up Snow White and tap in a highlight on the right side. Add tiny comma strokes of Antique Gold Deep sideloaded in Snow White. Complete petal 12 as above.

For petal 13, push out the edge in Snow White and use the dark mix to sweep through.

When all is dry, dry-brush Snow White on the front of petal 12.

Fluffy pink daisies Apply the pattern using the chalk method and use the same mixes as for the pink peony. Load the brush in Clear Glazing Medium, and wipe in the dark mix. Lay the first row of petals down using comma strokes. Wipe in the Glazing Medium again, and wipe in dark mix, then the light mix. Start this second row of petals just in from the tips of the first row. Wipe in Glazing Medium again, and wipe in the

light mix. Start this next row just in from the tips of the previous row. For the next few rows wipe the brush in Clear Glazing Medium, then wipe in a small amount of Snow White, holding the white to the surface. If the contrast is too great between rows sweep through the light mix on the opposite side to the white and place the white to the surface.

Wipe the brush, sweep in the light mix, then sideload in Snow White and place in all the little comma strokes around the centre. Keep them light. Tap in the centre with Antique Gold Deep, then tap the dark mix around the bottom half of the centre and Snow White in a circle in the middle.

Yellow daisies Push out the edge in Snow White. Wipe the brush and sweep through Antique Gold Deep, then Yellow Light, and pull the white down. Repeat for all the petals. The centre is Antique Gold Deep tapped in with a sideload of the dark pink mix and a highlight of Snow White tapped around the middle.

Rosebuds Load the brush in the dark pink peony mix, sweep through Snow White and with the white to the surface make two fat blobs side by side. Wipe the brush, sweep in the leaf mix, then sweep through Antique Gold Deep and paint the two outer sepals and the calyx. Sweep through a small amount of Snow White and with the white to the surface place in the middle stroke.

Forget-me-nots Place out on the palette one puddle of Snow White and one puddle of Blue Violet. Load the brush fully in Blue Violet, then tap into a little white. Place five small dabs down to form a flower. This is the dark colour, so do all these flowers first, placing them randomly throughout the spray. Don't wipe the brush but tap into more white and place more flowers down.

They should be lighter than the previous ones. Do the same again for the very lightest flowers. The dark flowers have Antique Gold Deep sideloaded in Snow White centres, while the lighter ones have Yellow Light sideloaded in Snow White. Place the tip of the brush towards the light source (or towards the top right-hand corner) and push in that direction. The result will be a tiny dot with a white highlight towards the top. These dots work best if the brush is bloated with paint, because you will get a nice rounded edge on them. Practise first. They look easy but are rather difficult to master. Add tiny leaves of leaf mix, then leaf mix swept through Yellow Light, then leaf mix, sweep Yellow Light, sweep Snow White.

Stand back from your piece and decide whether you need any more wash leaves. Now is the time to add them.

Edging Trace the smaller edge design around the inside of the tray. The large edge design is painted around the outside edge and down the folding legs. Use Glorious Gold.

Varnish with your favourite varnish, building up to six coats for protection against alcohol spills.

Farmyard cupboard

Pattern on pages 86–89

This cupboard, like the Schrank on page 62, was made by my father. It's made from pine and is 149 cm high by 43.5 cm wide by 40 cm deep (58½″ × 17″ × 15¾″). The bottom section of the cupboard tilts forward and conceals a kitchen tidy-bin. The top section has a storage shelf.

This design could also be used on facing cupboard doors. Or you could take individual sections of the design and place them around a trunk, across a pelmet, around a table top, or on a set of chair backs.

Palette (DecoArt Americana colours)
Sand
Williamsburg Blue
Snow White
Midnite Green
Evergreen
Dark Chocolate
Rookwood Red
Ebony Black
True Ochre
Yellow Light
Russet
True Red
Buttermilk
Raw Umber
an ordinary wax candle
Burnt Umber oil paint

Take the candle and rub it randomly all over the sides and top of the cupboard and *around* the doors. Don't rub it on the doors themselves. The water-based paints will not adhere to the waxed areas, leaving the wood showing through.

Sides   Paint the panels on the sides of the cupboard in Sand. Paint the panel surrounds Williamsburg Blue + Sand 2:1. You will probably need only one coat to cover. Now take a paint scraper and scrape up and down the areas that have the candle wax under them. Some of the paint should peel off leaving the woodgrain visible. (You may like to practise on an old piece of wood first, and experiment with different thicknesses of wax.)

Door surrounds   Paint the door surrounds Williamsburg Blue + Sand 2:1. Dry. Mask off 3 cm (1¼″) panels in the centre of all the door surrounds (sides, top, middle and bottom). Burnish the edges to prevent leakage—I usually use an eraser. Give these central areas one coat of Sand. Dry, and apply the pattern for the rose in the little squares left by the overlap of the masking tape. The roses are painted Rookwood Red with Snow White commas and dots.

Doors   The two doors are prepared the same way. Place out on a palette Williamsburg Blue, Sand and Snow White. Using a stiff 2.5 cm (1″) pastry brush pick up random amounts of the colours, one at a time, and criss-cross them over the door to form the background (or sky) area (see detail photographs). Keep the colours light as the border is painted with the same colours, used a bit darker. Dry overnight.

I left the area around the door with the leaf and rose motif on it until I had finished painting the rest of the design, but you may prefer to do all your basecoating at the one time. Mask off around the doors, leaving 3 cm (1¼″) around all four sides. Mask off 12 mm (½″) strips between the three design elements on each door. Remember to put the tape *on* the design area. Use a craft knife and ruler to cut out overlapping bits of tape. Using Williamsburg Blue, Sand and Snow White, criss-cross the paint onto the masked-off areas, keeping them darker, by picking up more Williamsburg Blue, than the inside area. As soon as the painting is finished carefully remove the masking tape. Dry thoroughly.

You may like to mask off the sides and bottom of each panel when you basecoat in the grass, but be certain to remove the masking tape as soon as you have finished painting or you may pull off bits of the background colour. Masking tape seems to develop extra 'stick' if left on too long. Apply the pattern for the grass to all six panels and block it in using a mix of Midnite Green + Evergreen 1:1. You will need a few coats. It can be a little streaky, but keep your brushstrokes running horizontally.

Top door
Barn design   Apply the pattern for the barns and tree. Block in the barns with Rookwood Red, and the roofs, barn doors, windows and weathervanes with Ebony Black. Mix a little Ebony Black into the Rookwood Red and wash in a shadow between the barn and the lean-to. The hay in the hayloft is painted with True Ochre, then True Ochre + Yellow Light, then Yellow Light + Snow White. Outline doors, hayloft and under the eaves with True Ochre. Paint a tiny triangle on the tower with True Ochre. The barn doors have Snow White crosses

40

on them. The tree has a streaky Dark Chocolate trunk with Evergreen leaves. Dab True Ochre over the middle of the leaves. Outline loosely with Midnite Green.

Bull   Trace on the patterns for both bull and sun and block in the bull in Sand. You will need three or four coats. Retrace the pattern, including all the direction lines. Make two values of the following mix: Raw Umber + Ebony Black + Snow White, to make a mid grey; to some of this mix add more Snow White. Use these two values to shade in the bull, building up depth as required. Use the lighter mix in the lighter areas, and the darker mix in the dark areas. Don't hurry this step—take your time. Mix Raw Umber + Ebony Black and paint the eye. Add Snow White to this mix and paint in the eyelid. Mix True Ochre + Raw Umber + a little Snow White and wash in the bags under his eye. The ear is the darker grey mix with Ebony Black + Raw Umber for the hairs. The horns are the dark grey mix with Snow White highlights, outlined with the Raw Umber + Ebony Black mix. Nostrils and mouth are Ebony Black. Hooves are the dark grey mix highlighted with Snow White. Place an Ebony Black line on them to indicate the two parts. When dry, dry-brush Snow White highlights onto the body and face. You will need to work at building up their intensity.

Moisten the area on the bull's forequarter where the spots are to go and, using Raw Umber and the tip of the round brush, touch the tip to the dampened surface to get soft washy spots.

Sun   Block in the area with True Ochre. Dab on True Ochre for the rays, then Yellow Light, then Snow White. Base the eye socket in Sand. Shade across the top of the socket and down the side of the nose with Russet. Outline across the top of the eye and the eyelid with a mix of Rookwood Red + Ebony Black. The eyebrows are this mix also. Eyeball is Russet with an Ebony Black pupil and a Snow White highlight. Paint a fine Ebony Black line across the bottom of the socket. Place dots on the inner edge of the eye in Rookwood Red. The nose is a stroke of Sand. Place a smaller stroke of Snow White down the middle of the nose, across the tip, under the nose above the top lip, and two strokes to form the chin. The lips are Rookwood Red. Dry-brush Sand, then Snow White, across the forehead and down the sides of the circle. Cheeks are Rookwood Red washed in. You will need to repeat this a few times. Dry. Place a Snow White highlight on the top of the cheeks.

Weeds   Mix Sand with Midnite Green and pull out tiny strokes with the liner brush.

Sheep   Mix True Ochre + Ebony Black + Snow White to make a warm light grey. Base the sheep in this mix. Paint the legs Ebony Black. Shade the face and inside the ear with Ebony Black + a touch of Raw Umber (keep mixing Raw Umber into the black until the black becomes a softer colour). Fill in the eye area with Snow White. Mix a tiny amount of Ebony Black into Snow White and paint the eyelid. Outline the eye and eyelid in Ebony Black. Iris is Ebony Black with a Snow White highlight.

To paint the fleece, mix Sand + Snow White to make a warm white. Starting around the neck area pull long strokes down towards the bottom of the fleece. Keep building up the texture. Remember this piece is antiqued so lots of texture looks great. Dry. Now work on the fleece with Snow White, using the same technique and letting some of the previous colour show through. Keep building up the texture.

Tulips   The two outside petals are True Ochre, the middle one is True Ochre tipped in Snow White. Leaves and stems are Midnite Green + Snow White.

Bottom door

Chickens   These are both painted the same. Mix Rookwood Red + True Red and base in the wattle and comb. The beak is True Ochre outlined in a mix of Rookwood Red + Ebony Black (dark warm brown). The eye is a True Ochre dot with a smaller Ebony Black dot in the centre. Place a Snow White highlight in the middle. Fill in the neck area with a mix of Buttermilk + Snow White. Base in the body with Rookwood Red. Recoat, this time mixing a little Ebony Black into the Rookwood Red to shade down the chest area and under the wings. While this is wet pick up True Ochre and place in the feathers on the tail and body. Dry. Now go back to the neck area and dry-brush the Buttermilk mix down on to the body to represent feathers. The legs are True Ochre for the front one and True Ochre + a tiny touch of Ebony Black for the one behind. Outline legs with the Rookwood Red + Ebony Black mix.

Daisies   Midnite Green stems and leaves. The petals are True Ochre tipped in Snow White. Place a Rookwood Red dot in the centre.

Cow   Base the cow in Sand. You will need at least three coats, with no ridges. Mix Rookwood Red + True Red + Snow White and paint in the udder. Now reapply the pattern with old Saral.

Mix Snow White + True Ochre + Ebony Black to make a warm grey. Use this mix to wash in the shade areas—underneath the tummy, around the udder, to separate the legs from the body, under the chin, and on the nose. The markings or splotches on the coat are washed in with Ebony Black. Work one area at a time,

having some areas lighter and some darker. The hooves and the nose are Ebony Black highlighted with Snow White. Outline the eye and place in the pupil with Ebony Black. Stroke on True Ochre on top of the eye socket and underneath the eye. Paint the insides of the ears with the grey shade mix, and the outsides with shade mix + Snow White. Outline with Ebony Black. Base the horns in Sand. Shade down the underneath of the horns with the shade mix and highlight with Snow White. Dry-brush Snow White highlights on the body and face. You will need to do this a few times to build up the intensity.

Weeds   Mix Sand with Midnite Green and pull out tiny strokes with the liner brush.

Wind cloud   Apply the pattern for the outline only— no face yet. Using the shade mix from the cow, base in the cloud loosely, using strokework. Pick up Sand and work that over the shade mix, then do the same with Snow White. Try and build up texture. Don't wash the brush when picking up colours. For the cloud underneath the face area, keep applying Snow White to get lots of texture. Dry and apply the face pattern. The eyebrows are Ebony Black. Wash in Russet below the eyebrows and down the sides of the nose. Mix Williamsburg Blue + Sand and base in the eye socket. Use this mix to wash some blue areas on the sides of the clouds, and also on either side of the cheeks. The cheeks and lips are Rookwood Red. You may need two or more coats on the cheeks, but keep them washy. The top eyelid is Sand, outlined in Ebony Black. The iris is Russet, the pupil Ebony Black with a Snow White highlight. Place the dot at the inner corner of the eye in Russet. For the nose, whisk the Williamsburg Blue mix down the centre, and when dry highlight with Snow White. Place tiny dots for the nostrils and outline the

end of the nose with a very fine line of Ebony Black. Using the same Williamsburg Blue mix, dry-brush in a straight line from the centre of the mouth for the 'breath'. Repeat with Snow White. Add some washy areas with True Ochre to the background clouds.

Pigs   These pigs are 'belted', which means they have a white band around their bodies. You may choose not to have the belts, but I rather like the effect. Base in the pig with a mix of Ebony Black + Raw Umber. Make sure it's still very dark but not quite black. Dry-brush Snow White along the back to highlight. Wash on some highlights with Snow White along the nose, under the chin and around the back leg. The belt or stripe is washy Snow White. Mix Snow White + Ebony Black and paint the nose. Add an Ebony Black dot for the nostril. The eye is Snow White with Ebony Black pupil and outlines.

Snowdrops   Leaves are Midnite Green + Snow White. Add tiny dots of Snow White for the petals.

Leaf and rose borders   Use the grass mix (Midnite Green + Evergreen) and paint in all the leaves and stems, keeping them casual. The roses are Rookwood Red with Snow White commas and dots.

Antique the finished piece using Burnt Umber oil paint.

You will not be able to apply a varnish to the waxed areas. I have paste-waxed the sides of my cupboard instead which gives a wonderful effect. Use a good quality furniture polish such as Busy Bee Beeswax or Gumleaf Natural Wood Polishing Wax. You can varnish the doors with your favourite varnish because they don't have wax on them.

Rooster cupboard

Pattern on pages 90–93

This cupboard is made from pine so it lends itself beautifully to distressing. Some of the grain is visible after the sanding which adds to the interest. The cupboard is 120 cm high by 61 cm wide, and is 40 cm deep (47¼″ × 24″ × 15¼″).

These designs would also suit a two-door cupboard and large trays.

Palette (Jo Sonja colours)
Topcoat mix: Warm White + Smoked Pearl 5:1. Make enough to paint the entire cupboard.
Border mix: The routed edge border around the rooster panels is also painted with Warm White + Smoked Pearl but in the ratio 1:1.

Warm White
Smoked Pearl
Red Earth
Teal Green
Amethyst
Paynes Grey
Pthalo Green
Burnt Sienna
Yellow Oxide
Antique Gold
Burnt Umber
Nimbus Grey
Napthol Crimson
Brilliant Green
Norwegian Orange
Cadmium Yellow Mid
Yellow Light
Carbon Black
Napthol Red Light
Green Oxide
Matisse Burgundy
large housepaint brush
size 8 filbert brush
coarse pastry brush or old flat brush, 2.5 cm (1″)

Using a large housepaint brush and Red Earth, roughly basecoat the entire cupboard. Don't try and cover the surface evenly, rather miss bits so the woodgrain is still visible. Dry, but don't sand. Paint the surface with one coat of the topcoat mix. Dry. Paint around the routed edge using the border mix. Using a hand sander (or lots of muscle) sand down the entire cupboard. Please wear a mask when sanding and work outside if possible. Sand with the grain, not across it, otherwise the scratch marks will show.

Start sanding with coarse paper, moving down through the grades until the surface feels smooth. Take off the paint along the edges of the door and around the routed panels. Sand hard in some areas to go through to the grain. When you are satisfied with the result wipe the cupboard over with a damp cloth to collect the dust.

The panels are painted with the criss-cross background technique described on page 11, using a 2.5 cm (1″) coarse pastry brush. (An old flat brush will do, as long as the brush marks from the coarse hairs are visible in the paint.) Put out a puddle of Smoked Pearl and an equal amount of Warm White. Using the stiff brush pick up a fair amount of Smoked Pearl on one side of the brush and about the same amount of Warm White on the other. Using criss-cross strokes, apply the paint over the surface. Pick up more paint every few strokes. Aim for a little texture, not great channels. The colour work-ups for the Pansies bedhead (page 72), Clock (page 27), Rooster cupboard (page 45) and Farm cupboard (page 38) all use this background technique, so refer to them also.

Upper door panel

Background Using old transfer paper, trace on only the hills and the tree. Using Amethyst + a little Paynes Grey wash in the most distant hill. Keep the background soft and indistinct. The next hill is Green Oxide, and the one in front is Teal Green with a little Pthalo Green added. The foreground is randomly streaked with Red Earth, Paynes Grey and Yellow Oxide. Dry-brush a little Pthalo Green as well. The tree has a Burnt Sienna trunk with Yellow Oxide leaves. Add touches of Green Oxide.

Trace off the rooster, placing in all the direction lines for the feathers.

Legs Base in Yellow Oxide. The two rear claws are Yellow Oxide + Burnt Sienna. Nails are Warm White. Recoat the legs. Work wet in wet, this time shading under the feathers at the top of the leg with Burnt Sienna, and highlighting with Warm White + Yellow Light placed in a brick pattern. Outline all in watery Carbon Black.

Comb and wattle Mix Burgundy and Red Earth and block in. Add a little Carbon Black to this mix and use

this to add some shade lines.

Beak Block whole beak in with Yellow Oxide. Recoat the top half of the beak with Yellow Oxide, highlighting with Warm White + Yellow Light. Add a little Burnt Sienna to the Yellow Oxide and base in the bottom half of the beak only. Outline in watery Carbon Black.

Eye Mix Napthol Red Light + Yellow Light and base in. Outline the eye with a mix of Napthol Red Light + Carbon Black. Pupil is Carbon Black. Highlight is a white dot to the right of the pupil.

Feathers Please refer to the pattern for the number sequence. The feathers on top of the legs (1) are a mix of Antique Gold + Burnt Umber. Recoat. Using a dirty brush dry-brush a little white on the right side to highlight. Using Burnt Umber block in the dark area of the body (2), all the way up the neck to the wattle. Recoat.

While still wet, sideload the brush in Warm White and place in the feathers around the neck (3) and down onto the chest. Add touches of Antique Gold and Yellow Oxide. The feathers near the tail (4) are Warm White, then Warm White sideloaded in Yellow Oxide.

For the flat feathers on the body (5) you will need a filbert brush. It is important to refer to the colour work-up sheet here. Load the brush in Burnt Umber and place in the stroke. You will be working wet in wet so do only a few feathers at a time. Wipe the brush, don't wash, and wipe in Warm White. This stroke sits over the Burnt Umber one. Start the stroke a little up from the end of the Burnt Umber and pull through. Practise a little before you work on your piece. Reverse the colours here and there. With the same dirty brush place a few strokes on the dark body of the rooster for highlights.

The small back feathers (6) are painted using Burnt Umber, Yellow Oxide and Antique Gold. Use these on their own as well as sideloading some strokes with

Workup for rooster cupboard

used the greens instead). The barn walls are Warm White, the roof and doors Red Earth. Outline the doors and roof with watery Carbon Black. The tree uses the same colours as before. The stone wall is painted in Yellow Oxide, Yellow Oxide + Burnt Sienna, Warm White, Warm White + Burnt Umber. Outline some rocks with watery Burnt Umber + Warm White. The path is Burnt Sienna; again, keep it watery.

Wash in a dark area across the front of the panel where the rooster will stand. Dry. Trace on the rooster, placing in the direction lines for the feathers.

Beak Mix Carbon Black + Napthol Red Light to make a dark red and base in the inside of the beak. The outside of the beak is Yellow Oxide.

Comb and wattle Mix Napthol Crimson + Red Earth and base in. Dry-brush a little Warm White for highlights. Shade with Burnt Umber down the middle of the wattle and around the beak. The wattle has a Warm White area on it shaded with Burnt Umber.

Eye Outline with Burnt Umber. Iris is Yellow Oxide with a Carbon Black pupil. Place a Warm White highlight to the right side.

Legs Yellow Oxide shaded with Burnt Sienna. Claws are Warm White. Highlight legs with Warm White + Yellow Oxide.

Body Block in neck area with Red Earth. Block in lower body with Matisse Burgundy, pulling little strokes along the top of the legs to represent feathers. Recoat and while wet add strokes of Paynes Grey. Dry-brush Norwegian Orange to separate the legs. Come back to the neck area (1) and place in feathers with Norwegian Orange, then Norwegian Orange sideloaded with Paynes Grey. As you move across the back towards the tail pick up Cadmium Yellow Mid. Overlap the feathers onto the body.

Tail Block in the area under the tail with Paynes Grey. Start pulling the feathers (2) with Paynes Grey sideloaded with Matisse Burgundy, Amethyst or Cadmium Yellow Mid (one colour at a time). Dry-brush on Brilliant Green. Keep checking on the direction of the feathers with your pattern.

Antique the finished project with Burnt Umber oil paint. When dry varnish with your favourite varnish—satin would be preferable.

Warm White. Add a few strokes of Burgundy + Red Earth.

The large tail feathers (7), and the topknot (8) are painted using Burnt Umber, Yellow Oxide, Warm White and Nimbus Grey. Again, some of these strokes can be sideloaded with Warm White as well as used on their own. When painting the topknot use very fine strokes and keep building up the colours.

Lower door panel
Using old Saral paper trace on the pattern for the hills, fence, barn and trees only. Using the same colours for the hills as before, casually wash these areas in (although I omitted the Amethyst hill in this section and

French influence screen

Pattern on pages 94–97

I tried to give an impression of faded elegance with this piece. The scrollwork and edges are 'worn', giving the screen a well-used appearance. I would have liked to sand down the floral swags to 'wear' them in as well, but couldn't bring myself to do it. You may have more courage!

The screen is made from 11 mm (⁷/₁₆″) craftwood. Each panel is 95 cm high and 40 cm wide (37½″ × 15¾″).

Other places these floral swags look good include bedheads, wardrobe doors, trunks and chests of drawers.

If any of the techniques in the following instructions are unfamiliar, please reread *The Next Step in Folk Art* pages 10–12, Glossary of Brush Loading Techniques.

Palette (Matisse colours)
Matisse have wonderful background colours in their range which already have sealer in them. Do not get them confused with the tube colours. Antique Blue and Antique Green are available in both ranges but are *not* the same colours. In the instructions I have written B for background, or T for tube, after the colour to prevent confusion.

Trim colour: Antique Blue (B) + Antique Green (B) +
 Pale Beige (B) (1:1:1)
Midnight Blue
Hooker's Green
Raw Sienna
Antique Green (T)
Antique White
Antique Blue (T)
Red Oxide
Ash Pink
Antique Gold

Basecoat the entire surface with Pale Beige (B). You will
need five or six coats. Sand lightly in between coats.
Measure in 3 cm (1¼") from the edges and mask off,
burnishing the edges to prevent leakage. I usually run
an eraser over the edge of the masking tape a few times.
Using a 2.5 cm (1") flat brush, casually apply one coat
of Trim mix to the edges. It will be streaky and a little
uneven but that's OK. Apply the pattern for the scrollwork. You may like to use a long liner brush for the
linework here. Outline the scrolls with Midnight Blue,
thinning the paint and loading the brush up to the
ferrule. As soon as the outlines are dry thin some Midnight Blue with water and fill the scrolls in. Dry. Now
take a water-moistened cloth and gently wipe some of
the paint off. Scary! You should still be able to see the
scrollwork but the lines should appear faded. Dry.

Apply the swag pattern with old Saral paper. I have not
included the wash leaves in the pattern because it is
easier to freehand them in.

Ring   The back of the ring is a mix of Red Oxide +
Raw Sienna. The front of the ring is Raw Sienna with
an Antique White highlight.

Leaves   Brush-mix Midnight Blue, Hooker's Green and
Raw Sienna. Add a little water to keep the paint transparent. Try and keep your strokes casual. As you are not
aiming for opaque colour, brushstrokes are fine. Place
a small stroke of Antique Green (T) on one side of the
leaves.

Wash leaves   Add these behind the design, keeping the
flow of the design in mind. Mix Midnight Blue +
Antique Blue (T) + Antique Green (T) to casually wash
these in. Thin the paint with water and keep them transparent. Outline some with thicker paint.

Roses   (see Step by Step on page 14)
Small roses: Mix Red Oxide + Ash Pink to make a deep
soft pink. Place in the fan-out centre (see page 10) using
the pink mix with a spot of Red Oxide near the ferrule.
Push out with Antique White and pull down with the
pink mix.
Large rose on centre panel: Place in the fan-out centre
using Ash Pink and the pink mix from the small rose for

2 1
8 7
6
11
10 3
12
5 4
9

the spot near the ferrule. Push out the edge with Antique White and pull down with Ash Pink. The front petal on the body of the rose, and the front petal on the skirt, are both pushed out in Antique White *and* pulled down with Antique White. When you have completed the body of the rose, take the pink mix and place a line around the edge of the body of the rose, where the skirt is going to be attached. This will add depth to this area. Don't pull your strokes in tight to the body, rather leave a small line of the pink mix showing through. All roses have tiny Antique Gold and white dots in the centres.

Large tulip   The painting sequence is numbered on the pattern, which you should keep in front of you for reference. Push out the edge in Antique White and pull down with Raw Sienna and Red Oxide. You can brush-mix these. Remember to keep the Red Oxide in the shade areas, that is, where petals overlap, and behind flipbacks. The vein lines are in Red Oxide.

Cup flowers   There are three types:
1. Pink cup flowers: Push out the back petal edge in Antique White. Wipe in the pink mix, and pull the colour down. Link up the front petal to the back with Antique White. Use the pink mix + Antique White to pull the front petal down.
2. Yellow cup flowers: Push out the edge in Antique White and use Raw Sienna to pull the white down.
3. Double pink cup flowers: There are two of these, one on each side panel. Push out the edge in Antique White and pull the strokes down with the pink mix.

Centre dots are Red Oxide, then Red Oxide + Antique White.

Rosebud   Push out with Antique White and pull down with pink mix.

Hanging flower   Push out the edge with Antique White, pull down the strokes with Raw Sienna. Calyx is leaf mix.

Tiny tulips   There are two types, red and yellow. For the red ones use Red Oxide for the two outside petals, then sweep in Antique White for the middle two. Hold the white to the surface.

For the yellow tulips, use Raw Sienna for the two outside petals, then sweep Antique White for the two middle petals.

Large yellow daisy (on end panels)   The back petals are Raw Sienna. As you move towards the front sweep in Antique White. Centre is Raw Sienna, then Raw Sienna + Antique White.

Blue daisies   First Midnight Blue, then sweep in Antique White. Hold the white to the surface. Centres are Antique Gold and Antique White.

Filler flowers   Antique White with a Red Oxide dot in the centre.

Stems   Use the dark leaf mix, sweeping through a little Antique White if needed to highlight.

Bow   To paint the bows appearing in the outer corners of the screen, use the edge mix (trim colour) and side-load in Antique White.

Let the screen dry overnight before you antique it. Wipe the Patina mix over the entire surface and antique lightly with Burnt Umber oil paint behind the swag and around the edges. I tried to give the effect of handmarks around the edges. When the antiquing is dry varnish with your favourite varnish.

I used Rub'n'Buff in Gold Leaf colour around the edges and on the trim as a final touch.

Cherub screen

Pattern on pages 98–100

The dimensions of this screen are the same as the French Influence Screen on page 48.

On this piece the richness of the imitation woodgrain has led me to keep decoration to a minimum. The faux woodgrain is great fun and very quick and easy to do.

If you don't feel up to painting the cherub, just paint the circlet of flowers.

Other ideas tor this design:

Across a bedhead. Repeat the tassels only on the foot

Across a chest of drawers

On a drawer front, with the tassels looped around the knobs

Across a fireplace mantel with the tassels hanging down either side

Paint the tassels on a wall above a painting or photograph

Use the cherub on a chairback

Palette (Matisse colours)
Red Oxide
Burnt Sienna
Ash Pink
Antique White
Chromium Green Oxide
Ultramarine Blue
Burnt Sienna
Titanium White
Midnight Blue
Metallic Light Gold
Burnt Umber

Napthol Scarlet
Antique Blue
Yellow Light
Burnt Umber
Mars Black
Antique Gold
Napthol Crimson
Raw Sienna
Metallic Gold
Drying Retarder

Faux woodgrain

First basecoat the screen with Red Oxide. You will need two coats.

The picture below illustrates the steps.

Step 1 Mix Yellow Light with enough water to make it runny. Using paper towel pat the watery Yellow Light onto the Red Oxide background. (Work one panel at a time.) Keep the colour splotchy and don't try to cover the entire surface. There is a lot of work to go over this. Take a 2.5 cm (1'') flat brush and using the same watery Yellow Light pull diagonal 'stripes' over the surface, flipping the brush from side to side. Do this quickly and don't try to make them even.

Step 2 Mix Napthol Scarlet with a little less water than you mixed in with the Yellow Light. The proportions are not critical. All you need to do is reduce the consistency to make the paint more workable and reduce its opacity. Crumple a sheet of newspaper into a ball. Dab it into the watery red mix and pounce it over the surface. Move your hand about so you don't get a repeating pattern. Dry.

Step 3 Mix Burnt Umber + Burnt Sienna 1:1. Add a few drops of Drying Retarder and a small amount of water until the mix has the consistency of pouring cream. Take a sponge brush and paint this mix over the surface. Do only one surface at a time (e.g. if you are working on a box or trunk complete this step on one side before going on to the next). Don't let the paint mix dry at this stage. If you feel it is drying too quickly add more retarder and repaint the entire area. Take another sheet of newspaper and fold it diagonally, then roll it up loosely. Starting at one corner, roll the paper diagonally across your piece. Repeat all the way down. If you accidentally bump your hand onto the wet surface and make a mark (as I did), apply a small amount of the paint mix and re-roll that area. Dry overnight. If you would like a darker effect, repeat the last step.

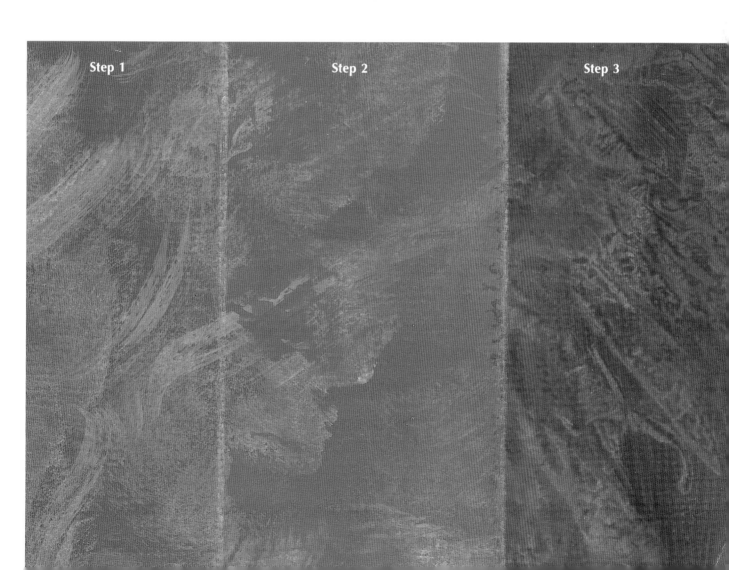

pink, not sunburnt. Base in the cherub using smooth strokes. You will need four or more coats. Dry. To some of this mix add a little Red Oxide to make a shade colour for the darker areas of the skin.

2. Using a very sharp pencil and old Saral paper, trace on the facial features and all the finger, foot and crease lines. Using watery Red Oxide outline the facial features carefully with very fine lines.

3. Using the shade mix, shade down the left side of the face, washing away any hard edges. Shade down the left side of the nose and under the tip of the nose.

4. Base in the eye area with Antique White.

5. Mix Red Oxide with a little Antique White + a tiny touch of Napthol Scarlet and paint in the lips. The teeth are Antique White. Outline again with Red Oxide if necessary. Place small highlights in the middle of the upper and lower lips.

6. Using Antique White highlight the tip of the nose and the nostrils. Keep the left side very small.

7. Dry-brush Antique White across the forehead, under the eyes and onto the cheekbone area, keeping it mainly on the right side.

8. Feather in the eyebrows using Red Oxide.

9. Shade under the lips where the lips recede, then highlight the dimple in the chin with Antique White. Dry-brush Napthol Scarlet + Antique White across the cheeks and under the highlight on the cheek bone.

Eyes

1. Base in the iris with Yellow Oxide.

2. Add a Burnt Umber pupil.

3. Mix Ultramarine Blue + Burnt Umber + Antique White and paint in the iris.

4. Add a hard Antique White highlight to the right of the pupil, and a soft secondary highlight on the lower left.

5. Outline the eye again with Red Oxide, this time adding a lower lid crease.

6. Add a tiny amount of black to the blue mix used for the iris. Shade underneath the top eyelid, on the eye itself, to sink this area back.

7. Add eyelashes with a mix of Burnt Umber + Mars Black.

Hair

1. Using the skin shade mix wash in the areas around the face that will be under the hair.

2. Loosely base in the hair with Yellow Oxide.

3. Recoat.

4. Add wisps of hair using the following colour combinations:
   Yellow Oxide + Antique White
   Yellow Light
   Yellow Light + Antique White
and for the darker areas use Burnt Sienna.

Oval

Centre the pattern on your piece. I placed mine 16 cm (6¼") down from the top of the panel.

1. Trace a line through the middle of the circlet of roses. Base this oval in with Ash Pink. You will need at least two coats.

2. Using a large soft flat brush pick up Antique Blue and slip-slap this around the edge of the oval. You may prefer to moisten the area with water first to make blending a little easier.

3. Pick up Antique White and slip-slap that on as well, blending where the two colours meet. Add more Antique White as you move into the centre.

4. Dry, and trace on the pattern for the cherub, omitting the facial features.

Cherub

When I refer to the left and right side in the instructions I mean *your* left or right, not the cherub's.

1. Mix a warm skin colour using Antique White with a touch of Yellow Oxide and a touch of Napthol Scarlet. If you need to cool it down add a touch of Chromium Green Oxide. The baby cherub should be lovely and

Body

1. Using the skin shade mix, shade down all the extremities and under the chin. You will need to do this three or four times because you are only using soft washes of colour.

2. Highlight the chest with dry-brushing, as well as the right shoulder, both knees, the pads of the left foot and the side of the right one.

3. Wash Antique White onto the finger-pads and the bottom of the toe-pads.

4. Place in the belly-button using the skin shade mix.

Ribbon

1. Base in the entire ribbon with Ash Pink.

2. Indicate folds and crevices with a mix of Ash Pink + Red Oxide.

3. Add highlights with Antique White.

Try and work the ribbon wet in wet wherever possible and softly blend the colours.

4. Dry-brush on additional highlights when the work is dry.

55

Tendrils in the hair and hand Mix Yellow Light + a little Mars Black to make green. Use this to place in tiny comma strokes for the leaves, following the close-up photo. Add tiny blossoms with Ultramarine Blue + Napthol Scarlet + Antique White.

Stand back and assess your work. Remember you will be viewing this from a distance, so do all the highlights show up? Hold your work up to a mirror too. Any faults are glaringly obvious this way.

Rose border Trace on the pattern for the roses. I have only given you half the pattern, so turn it over and trace off for the other side. I find it easier to freehand the leaves in, but you may like to trace them in also.

Leaves Mix Yellow Light + Mars Black to make a dark Antique Green. Add a touch of Napthol Scarlet to this. Load the brush in this mix, sweep through Antique Gold, and paint in all the leaves. Keep them very small. Add stems with this mix also. The leaves on the side panels have knife strokes of leaf mix swept through Titanium White.

Roses

White roses (really pale grey)
Make the following mix:

Antique Gold	4 parts
Titanium White	2 parts
Mars Black	2 parts
Napthol Scarlet	1 part

Add a little Mars Black to some of this mix for the dark centre.

1. Refer to the roses step by step on page 14. Paint a circle using the light grey mix. Add a centre of the darker mix. I painted all the circles first, then all the centres.
2. Load the brush in the lighter grey mix, sweep through Antique Gold, then sweep through Titanium White. Turn the rose so that the darker centre is at the bottom and, with the white held to the surface, pull a comma stroke around the centre. Sweep through more Titanium White, hold the white to the surface and, with the tip of the brush overlapping the previous comma stroke, pull the next one around the other side. Turn the rose right way up, sweep through a little more Titanium White, hold the white now to the outside of the rose and pull three comma strokes for the skirt. Add tiny comma strokes in the centre. Because some of the roses are bigger than others, depending on the size of the centre add either 1, 2 or 3 commas. Add tiny dots of Antique Gold swept through Titanium White. Keep up on the tip of the brush.

Red roses
1. Using Raw Sienna, block in a circle.
2. Mix Napthol Scarlet + Mars Black to make a brick red colour and paint in the centre circle.
3. Load the brush in the red mix, sweep through Raw Sienna then sweep through Titanium White and, with the white held to the outside, push out three strokes around the centre circle.
4. Sweep through more Titanium White and, with the white held to the surface, place a comma stroke across the body of the rose. Wipe the brush.
5. Turn the work upside down, reload the brush, and push out the petals along the bottom of the rose.
6. Add tiny comma strokes in the centre, again depending on the size of the rose. Tip the brush in Titanium White and, keeping right up on the tip of the brush, paint a spiral in the centre.

Daisies

Blue daisies: Mix Midnight Blue + Antique Blue. Load the brush in this, sweep through Titanium White, and with the white held to the surface, place in the petals. Sideload into Titanium White, and with the white looking into the centre place push-dots along the bottom of the daisy. For the centre load the brush in Raw Sienna, sideload in Antique Gold, push the Antique Gold to the top of the daisy then lift off. For the tiny knife-stroke daisies, load the brush in the blue mix, sideload in Titanium White, and pull knife strokes down towards the stem.

Yellow daisies: These appear only on the side panels. Load the brush in Antique Gold then sweep in Titanium White.
  The centres are the same as for the blue daisies. Add comma strokes where necessary in the leaf mix, then sweep through Titanium White and place in some lighter ones, especially on the faux woodgrain. The daisy stems are painted with this also.

Large roses on the side panels

The white/grey rose on the bottom of the spray is painted exactly like the small ones.
Plum-coloured rose:
1. Mix Napthol Crimson with enough Mars Black to make a burgundy colour. You will need to add white to this to see the colour correctly. Base the circle in this.
2. Add a little more Napthol Crimson to the dark mix. Trace the pattern on again if required and push out the edge in Titanium White. Wipe the brush, sweep in the burgundy mix and pull the white down.
3. Repeat for the other side but increase the white on the front petal by sweeping through Titanium White as you near the front.
4. Repeat the same steps as before for the skirt.

5. Add Titanium White comma strokes in the middle.
6. Load the brush in Antique Gold, tip in Titanium White and place tiny dots in the centre.

Rope, tassels and knobs   Place the knob pattern for the side panels 27 cm (10½") down from the centre top. On the middle panel the knob is 2.5 cm (1") down from the top. Now take a 60 cm (24") length of rope or twisted cord and hold it over the middle knob. Position the other end on the side panel knob and let the cord drape softly and naturally. Ask someone to chalk along the line of the rope. The chalk line should tuck under the roses on the side of the oval. Trace the line off onto greaseproof paper, turn the paper over, and trace it onto the other side of the screen. If you tried to drape the rope on the other side you probably wouldn't get a match. Apply the pattern for the rest of the design.

Because of the similarity of the paint names I have used the following mixes:

Shade mix: Metallic Gold + Burnt Umber
Base colour: Metallic Gold
Highlight: Metallic Light Gold
Final highlight: Metallic Light Gold + Titanium White

Knobs   Base in the oval with the base colour. Shade around the edge with the shade colour. Recoat the oval and, starting at the outer edge and using the shade colour, walk the colour towards the centre. Don't go all the way to the centre. Wipe the brush, sweep through the highlight colour and repeat for the other side. Add a dab of final highlight colour on the left side. Load the brush in the base colour, sideload in the shade colour and with the shade colour against the oval, push out the fancy edge.

Rope   Load the brush in the base colour, sideload the brush on one side in the shade colour and on the other in the highlight colour. Paint a series of S strokes, always holding the shade colour to the bottom.

Tassels   Work one section at a time.
1. Block in this area with the base colour. Shade the right side using the shade colour and highlight using the highlight colour. Add a small final highlight in the middle of the right side.
2. Add a line of base colour, with a fine line of Burnt Umber just above it.
3. Block in this area with the base colour. Shade and highlight as before. Paint fine lines in Burnt Umber while the base colour is still wet. Add final highlights on the middle of the right side, only letting the paint wear off your brush as you move away from the area.
4. Load the brush as for the rope and paint S strokes.
5. Using Burnt Umber, shade underneath the S strokes, pulling the lines down into the fringe. Now starting from the bottom of the fringe pull fine lines of base colour up into the Burnt Umber. Don't go all the way to the S strokes with this colour. Add strokes of highlight colour, then a few on the right side of the final highlight colour.

Paint a Metallic Gold line all the way around the screen, 2.5 cm (1") in from the outside edge. Paint the cut edges Metallic Gold.

Antique the screen using Burnt Umber oil paint. Varnish with your favourite varnish.

The hinges used on the screen, called Uni hinges, move forward and backwards.

Topiary tree

(Sally's cupboard no. 2)

Pattern on pages 112–13

This cupboard matches the one my friend Sally helped me prepare for *The Next Step in Folk Art* (page 52).

The design could also be used on matching door panels or wardrobe doors, or be painted on the wall either side of a bedhead.

Palette (DecoArt Americana colours)
Flesh Tone
Enid's Collection
Brilliant Red
Antique Green
Antique Gold Deep
Blue Green
Snow White
Ebony Black
Sealer
Brush 'n' Blend
Burnt Umber oil paint

Seal the raw wood with one coat of sealer. Sand. Using a large 2.5 cm (1″) flat brush apply the Flesh Tone. You will probably need quite a few coats to give an opaque finish, but hang in there. When dry, sand lightly, apply the pattern for the pot and pole and paint in. Make certain you centre the pattern both vertically and horizontally.

Pole Mask down both sides of the pole with masking tape. Block in this area with Antique Gold Deep. Make certain it's opaque. Mix Brilliant Red and Antique Green to make a warm Burnt Sienna. Moisten one side of the pole with water and wash a fairly transparent line of the Burnt Sienna mix down the length of the pole. Try and bring the colour towards the middle so the pole will appear rounded, but keep an area in the centre free of the Burnt Sienna mix. You are only working in a small area so it's a little tricky. Repeat for the other side when this side has dried.

Pot Give the surface one coat of Antique Gold Deep. You should be able to still see the lines of the pattern. Work on the bottom section of the pot first. Recoat this area only and let dry. Apply another coat, then, using the same Burnt Sienna mix as on the pole, start at the edge and walk the colour across to the other side. You will find that you will only need a small amount of paint. When dry repeat for the other side.

You will notice I have left the centre of the pot free of Burnt Sienna. Recoat the rim area and shade that in the same way. I have also shaded under the rim on the body of the pot. Make sure this area is dry or you will pick up what you have already painted. Using the same Burnt Sienna mix recoat the back section of the pot. This area was done in Antique Gold Deep, and you will need a few coats.

Using Snow White dry-brush some highlights down the centre of the pot and rim. They should be very soft. Carefully tidy up any edges. Use Flesh Tone to restore the basecoat if needed.

Topiary top Apply the pattern to your piece using the chalk method and roughly mark in the outside perimeter of the design with a dotted line. This will be a guide for the wash leaves. Mix Antique Green + Ebony Black to make a dark green. Thin this with water and freehand in lots of wash leaves inside the dotted line. Extend a few leaves or comma strokes outside the line for interest. You don't want the tree to look as if it has just had a haircut! Keep the leaves drooping down and curve the stems in to the top of the pole. The idea is to fill up the area behind the pattern with soft leaves to add interest. Don't worry if your strokes aren't perfect; there is so much to go on top you won't even notice.

Leaves Mix Antique Green + Ebony Black to get the same dark green as before and paint in the leaves solidly. You will need two coats. Pull all the stems down to the top of the pole even though this isn't shown on the pattern.

Tulip leaves Give them one coat of the Antique Green + Ebony Black mix and let dry. Sideload in Antique Gold Deep for the second coat and let that dry.

Hydrangeas Apply the Brush'n'Blend to the pattern area. Don't wash the brush. Following the colour work-up, pick up a little Brilliant Red and wash that roughly over one side, then pick up a little Antique Green and do the same on the other. Wipe the brush, wipe in Snow White and, starting in the *middle* of the flower, place little groups of 3, 4 or 5 petals over the wet area. Try and keep the lightest colour near the centre. If you need to reload, go over the flowers in the middle again to take off some of the paint. Add tiny Brilliant Red and

Snow White dots in the centres of the middle flowers, and don't reload for the outside ones, keeping them soft and misty.

Roses Please refer to the step by step on page 14 for detailed instructions, but paint all three roses in the following colours: Mix Brilliant Red + Antique Green to make a dull red or Burnt Sienna mix. (Don't use the bottled Burnt Sienna as it is nothing like the Burnt Sienna you want here.) You will only need a small amount of Antique Green to dull the red—if you add too much it will end up brown. Fan out the centre using the Burnt Sienna mix, Antique Gold Deep and Ebony

Black. Push out the petals with Snow White, wipe the brush, wipe in Burnt Sienna mix, sweep in Antique Gold Deep and hold the Antique Gold Deep to the surface while pulling the strokes down. Repeat for all petals and the skirt. Add tiny Antique Gold Deep and Snow White dots in the centre. For the rose that is tilted forward (the highest one) paint the back petals first, before putting in the fan-out centre, then continue as before.

Cup flowers Push out the edge in Snow White. Wipe the brush, sweep through Blue Green, and pull the white down. For the hanging flower paint the bump at the back first. Add a small highlight with the dirty brush swept in Snow White.

Tulip   Load the brush in the same Burnt Sienna mix as before. Sweep through Antique Gold Deep and sideload in Snow White. With the white held to the right, paint an S stroke. Repeat for the other side, still keeping the white to the right. Sideload into more white and keeping the white to the right place in the outside centre strokes. Sideload in Snow White once again but hold the white to the surface while you pull the middle stroke through.

Rosebuds   Load the brush in the Burnt Sienna mix, sweep through Antique Gold Deep, then sweep through Snow White. Hold the white to the surface and paint a blob. You may need two blobs to fill the area. Wipe the brush load in the leaf mix (Antique Green + Ebony Black), sweep through Antique Gold Deep and paint the two outside leaves on the calyx. Using the same load on your brush, sweep through a little Snow White and pull the middle leaf through.

Filler flowers   Position these over the wash leaves as they tend to get lost on the Flesh Tone background colour. They are painted in Snow White with a Brilliant Red dot in the centre. All stems are the leaf mix swept through Antique Gold Deep.

Ribbon   Using the same Burnt Sienna mix as for the roses, sideload in Snow White and blend softly on the palette. Hold the white to the outside and complete the pattern.

Stand back and assess your piece as a whole. Add any wash leaves or filler strokes necessary to balance the design.

When dry, antique lightly with Burnt Umber oil paint. Dry, and varnish with your favourite varnish.

Schrank

Pattern on pages 101–111

This piece is based on the scaled-down dimensions of an antique German Schrank. (The German word *Schrank* means a cupboard in the kitchen, and a wardrobe in the bedroom. Thanks to Scottie Foster for this information.) As you can see from the before and after photographs it really is an amazing transformation. I hope it will inspire you to paint a large piece of furniture of your own.

I have based the design on a loose combination of styles after careful study of German and Austrian museum pieces. I was aiming for something lighter and more in keeping with today's decor than the heavier styles and colours of the past.

I hope future generations of our family will enjoy our work, as this piece was built by the loving hands of my father and painted with love and care by me. I have recorded all the paints and mediums used on this piece on its back, as a guide for future restorers. Perhaps when you are creating your next heirloom you might consider this also. See stockists' list for the pattern to make the Schrank.

I used Matisse paints for my heirloom because their paints and mediums are of the highest artist's quality, and they are made by an Australian family company.

Palette (Matisse colours)
Matisse supply an Antique Blue and an Antique Green in jars (background colours) and tubes. They are *different* colours. The background colours have a sealer already mixed into the paint.

Background colours (250 ml jars):
  Antique Blue
  Pale Beige

Tube colours:
  Antique White
  Antique Gold
  Antique Blue
  Burnt Sienna
  Burnt Umber
  Midnight Blue
  Titanium White
  Napthol Scarlet
  Yellow Light
  Mars Black
  Raw Sienna

Faux Finish and Marbling Gel
Pre-Antiquing Medium
Patina
High Gloss varnish (turps-based)
Matt varnish (turps-based)
Art Spectrum Burnt Umber Artist Quality oil paint
Jo Sonja's Tannin Blocking Sealer for Wood
Drying Retarder
large housepainting brush

Mixes:
Blue basecoat mix: Antique Blue (jar) + Pale Beige 2:1
Cream panel mix: Antique White + Pale Beige (jar) 1:1
Brown mix: Burnt Sienna + Burnt Umber 1:1

Apply the Tannin Blocking Sealer to any areas of the raw wood that are knotted or dark in colour. Apply undiluted with a soft dry brush, brushing the sealer out from the suspect area.

Using a large good quality housepainting brush apply the blue basecoat mix to one section at a time.

Act Justly Love Tenderly
Walk Humbly Micah 6:8

Philip   Michael   1994   Timothy   Leanne

in the cream mix. You will need two or three coats.

Refer to the section on Marbling on page 16 before marbling the carved edges (but not the routed edges on the door panels).

Scrolls and poles The poles on the edges of the large panels are all 1 cm (⅛'') wide, while the poles on the door panels are 7 mm (¼'') wide. Mask off these areas, again burnishing the edges to prevent leakage. Block in the poles using Antique Gold. You will need at least two coats. Allow to dry.

Using a large flat brush, moisten the surface of a pole with Drying Retarder. Load the brush in Antique Gold, then sideload in the brown mix, and stroke the brush back and forth on the palette to softly blend the colours together. Now hold the brown to the outside of the panel and run the brush down beside the masking tape. You will have to reload a number of times to cover the length. Blend the joins together by brushing over them a few times. Repeat the process for the inner side of the pole, using Titanium White for the sideload. Repeat the process for each pole in turn, and pull the masking tape off as soon as you have finished painting.

Basecoat the scrolls in Antique Gold, making sure to keep an even width all the way down. With Antique Gold in the brush, sideload in Titanium White and with the white looking to the right pull the stroke away from the beginning of the scroll and down to the other end, crossing in the middle to end up on the other side. Reload the brush and repeat from the other end of the scroll. Wipe the brush, load again in Antique Gold, sweeping through a little brown mix, and do the same as before. Keep carefully to the blocked-in area of the scroll as you don't want any added width. Repeat for each scroll in turn.

Vase Base in with Antique Blue (tube paint). Working on a section at a time, shade with Midnight Blue, using light washes to build up depth of colour. Keep the shade area to the right side of the vase. Using Titanium White dry-brush highlights down the left side, again working slowly to build up the highlight. When dry, trace the lines on the neck and body of the vase. Place a fine line along the traced edge of the design and dry-brush in the highlights. The handles are blocked in first with Antique Blue; then sideload into Midnight Blue and, keeping the Midnight Blue to the right side, pull a dark line down the handle. Repeat with Titanium White, holding the white to the left side of the handle. Dry-brush Titanium White on the foot of the vase.

Scroll above door The technique is the same as for the vase. Block in with Antique Blue (tube paint) and shade with Midnight Blue, washing in the shade areas. Dry-brush in the highlights. Outline the scroll in thinned

Let dry for a few minutes then take a water-dampened cloth and wipe off some of the paint. Rub back to the wood in a few areas for interest. You are aiming for a slightly transparent basecoat rather than an opaque cover, so one coat should suffice. Repeat for all areas, even those under the cream panels.

Panels beside the door Measure down 14 cm (5½'') from the top of the cupboard and centre the patterns for the cream panels on either side of the door. Mask off the area with masking tape, burnishing the edges to prevent leakage. Use the cream panel mix and basecoat in the panels. You will need a few coats to get an even finish. When dry, sand the area well with fine sandpaper until some of the blue basecoat starts to show through.

Door panels Centre the designs in the door panels, and mask and basecoat in the same way.

Side panels Measure 15 cm (6'') down from the top, and 15 cm (6'') in from the front, to position the patterns for the side panels. Mask off these areas also and block in.

Routed and carved edges Base in the routed edge on the door panels and the carved edges at top and bottom

Titanium White. Trace on the letters carefully and paint them in using unthinned Titanium White. Some of the letters may look a little odd, but this is characteristic of this type of lettering. Change it if it worries you (but personally I like things a little unusual).

Leaves (These instructions refer to all leaves throughout the design.) Block in the leaves with Midnight Blue, using only one coat. Wipe off a small part of each leaf, using the brush, to bring a highlight to the leaf. Where one part of a leaf overlaps another, as on the side panels, sweep through Antique Gold and highlight the top leaf.

All leaves have knife strokes of Midnight Blue swept through Antique Gold. Don't make them all the same. On some leaves put in a centre vein only, on others have two or three major veins. Add some wash leaves using water-thinned Midnight Blue. Remember when painting the design on the door panels to pull all the stems down to the neck of the vase. More can be added when the flowers have been painted.

Wash leaves   For the circlet on the side panels, trace on the design using the chalk method. Use the thinned Midnight Blue as before and, working in the one direction, place in the leaves, pulling them tight into the circle. Add a few small leaves moving in the other direction.

To paint the wash leaves in the swag on the door and in the trails down the poles, again use the thinned Midnight Blue and paint in soft flowing leaves, using your brush strokes to complete.

I find it easier to freehand the leaves in rather than to follow a pattern. Using a chalk pencil, give yourself a guide, then go for it. Once you start it really becomes easier.

Flower mixes

1. Yellow Light + a small amount of Mars Black to make an Antique Green.

2. Napthol Scarlet + a small amount of the Antique Green mix to make a warm red-brown or Burnt Sienna. Don't use the tube colour—it is too dark.

Tulips   Painted in two colours, red and yellow. Please refer to the French Influence Screen on page 48 for a step by step for the tulips.

Red tulips: These are on the top door panel, the side panels on the front and the panels on the side. Follow the numbers on the pattern for the petal painting sequence.

Push out the edge in Titanium White, wipe the brush, sweep through the Burnt Sienna mix, sweep through Raw Sienna, sweep through Yellow Light and with the Yellow Light held to the surface pull down the white. Wipe the brush, sideload into Titanium White, push out the edge and repeat as before. Add a little more Antique Green mix to the Burnt Sienna and pull tiny strokes up from the base of the tulip. Add veins with this mix also.

Yellow tulips: Again follow the pattern numbers and push out the edge in Titanium White, working one petal at a time. Wipe the brush, sweep through Raw Sienna then sweep through Yellow Light; with the Yellow Light held to the surface pull the white down. Pull Burnt Sienna mix lines up from the bottom.

Load the brush in Midnight Blue, sweep through Antique Gold and with the gold to the surface pull the stems in towards the vase or the centre of the design.

Crocuses   The crocuses on the front side panels and the hanging crocus on the top door are red. The two crocuses on the bottom door panel are yellow.

Hanging red crocus: Paint the hanging crocus on the top door panel first. Load the brush in the Burnt Sienna mix, sweep through Yellow Light, and paint in the four outside petals. Reload the brush as before, this time wiping the brush in a little Titanium White, and with the white to the surface pull through the middle petal. For the calyx, load the brush in Midnight Blue, sweep through a little Antique Gold and paint two S strokes on either side. Sweep through a little Titanium White and pull the middle stroke through.

Open red crocus: Load the brush in the Burnt Sienna mix, sweep through Yellow Light, then sweep through Titanium White. Hold the white to the side of the petal and with light pressure start the stroke. As you move into the middle of the petal apply heavier pressure to make the bristles spread, then release the pressure as you near the end of the stroke. Repeat for the other side. All the petals are painted in this way, reloading the brush each time. Load the brush in Burnt Sienna mix, sweep through Yellow Light then sweep through Titanium White, and pull fine knife strokes for the stamens.

Yellow crocus: Use the same technique as above, but use these colours: Load the brush in Raw Sienna, sweep through Antique Gold, then sweep through Yellow Light and lastly sweep through Titanium White. Proceed as above. For the stamens load the brush in the Burnt Sienna mix, then sweep through Antique Gold.

Yellow cup flowers and daisies   Push out the edge in Titanium White. Wipe the brush, load in Antique Gold, sweep through Yellow Light and with the Yellow Light to the surface pull the white down. For the centres of the daisies load the brush in Antique Gold then tip in Burnt Sienna and tap in an oval. Add a Titanium White highlight. The cup flowers have dots of Burnt Sienna mix, then Burnt Sienna mix and Yellow Light.

Rosebuds   Load the brush in the Burnt Sienna mix, sweep through Yellow Light and with the Yellow Light to the surface place in two blobs side by side. Wipe the brush, load in Midnight Blue, sweep through Antique Gold and with the gold to the surface place in the two outside sepals on the bud. Sweep the brush through a small amount of Titanium White and pull the middle sepal through. Load the brush in the blue again, sweep through the gold and with the gold to the surface paint another blob underneath the sepals. Use this same load to paint the stems.

Roses Follow the Step by Step for Roses on page 14 for detailed instructions, using the following colours: Fan out the centre using Burnt Sienna mix and Mars Black. Push out the edges in Titanium White. To pull down the white, load with the Burnt Sienna mix, sweep through Antique Gold and with the gold to the surface pull the white down. All the roses are painted using these colours. Mix only enough paint to do a few flowers at a time, rather than enough to complete the entire project at once. This will ensure slight variations in the colour mixes which will result in wonderful gradations of colour throughout the roses.

Lettering I have not included an alphabet as there are so many different styles of lettering available I felt you might like to make your own choice. Your local library would be a good source. I am, however, including general instructions on how to trace and paint your chosen letters. Another easy way of painting large letters is to purchase an alphabet stencil. These are cheap and are available from most craft stores.

Measure the width of the Schrank. Trace out the letters of each of the names that are going to appear at the foot of your heirloom, and the date. Measure the total length of the names and date without spacing gaps and deduct this measurement from the width of the Schrank. Now divide the remainder by the number of word spaces required, allowing for the names to start and finish a little way in from the edges, say, 3 cm (1¼''). Trace off the letters and numbers. Using Titanium White carefully block in each letter. (I found a size 4 flat brush worked best.) You will need two coats. Draw a chalk line just above halfway through the letters. Using this line as a guide, dry-brush on Antique Blue on the lower part of the letters.

If you want to include a lot of names, you may have to continue them evenly onto the sides of the Schrank.

Evaluate Stand back and assess the completed piece. Do you need to add more wash leaves to balance up one side with the other? Look for any paint smudges and rectify them now. Check that all the centres are in the roses. You are now ready for antiquing.

Antiquing Allow yourself three hours to complete this job. Work in a well ventilated area or outside and wear disposable rubber gloves. Have a good supply of clean lint-free cotton rags handy, cut into manageable sizes. Apply an even coat of Pre-Antiquing medium to the whole Schrank and let dry for an hour. (Because the binding qualities of the paint used in the wash leaves have been reduced by adding water to it, these leaves might start to fade or disappear during the antiquing process because of the rubbing action necessary to apply the Patina. The Pre-Antiquing medium provides a protective barrier between the painted surface and the Patina.)

Working one section at a time, apply the Patina all over the surface of the Schrank. In a shallow container squeeze out some Burnt Umber oil paint and add a small amount of Patina to it to make it workable. Antique in the usual fashion, darkening around the edges of the scrolls and down the length of the poles. Keep the colour on the marbled area fairly light. The raw wood areas will come up a little darker than the other areas, which is great. The sanded areas under the cream panels also become more noticeable.

When you have finished place all rags and gloves in a strong plastic bag, fill it with water, tie the top and place in an outside rubbish bin. A few cases of spontaneous combustion of rags have been known to occur but following these precautions will eliminate concern.

Varnishing In a clean container pour 125 cm (½ cup) of Gloss Finish and 125 ml (½ cup) of Matt Finish. Shake well. You now have a beautiful satin finish that is non-yellowing and quick-drying. I have chosen to use turps-based varnishes because they are completely strippable. If in one hundred years time an enthusiastic relative wants to restore my heirloom the varnish and all the accumulated grime can be removed with mineral turpentine *without* affecting the artwork. If you have used any brand of paint other than Matisse, please trial test a sample area first as acrylic brands vary.

Well done! You have just created your own family heirloom.

Pansies bedhead

Pattern on pages 114–115

This bedhead was a secondhand shop find, and cost just $10. My father sanded it down for me, and I gave the bare wood one coat of Jo Sonja's All Purpose Sealer before I started painting. You probably won't find a bedhead the same as this but the pattern will adapt itself to lots of different bedhead shapes.

This wreath of pansies could also be adapted for use on box lids, trays (omit bow), door panels, chair backs, chests of drawers and trunk ends.

Palette (Jo Sonja colours)
Antique Gold
Teal Green
Burgundy
Diox Purple
Sapphire
Ultra Blue Deep
Storm Blue

Moss Green
Warm White
Turner's Yellow
Cadmium Yellow Mid
Fawn
Amethyst
Carbon Black
Indian Red Oxide
Matisse Burgundy
(Note I have used two burgundies—Jo Sonja and Matisse)

Trace on the pattern with old Saral paper, omitting the wash leaves. These are best freehanded in. Keep the pattern in front of you to refer to if necessary.

Ribbon Using Storm Blue paint in the ring the ribbon is hanging from. Paint the ribbon in Jo Sonja Burgundy sideloaded with Warm White.

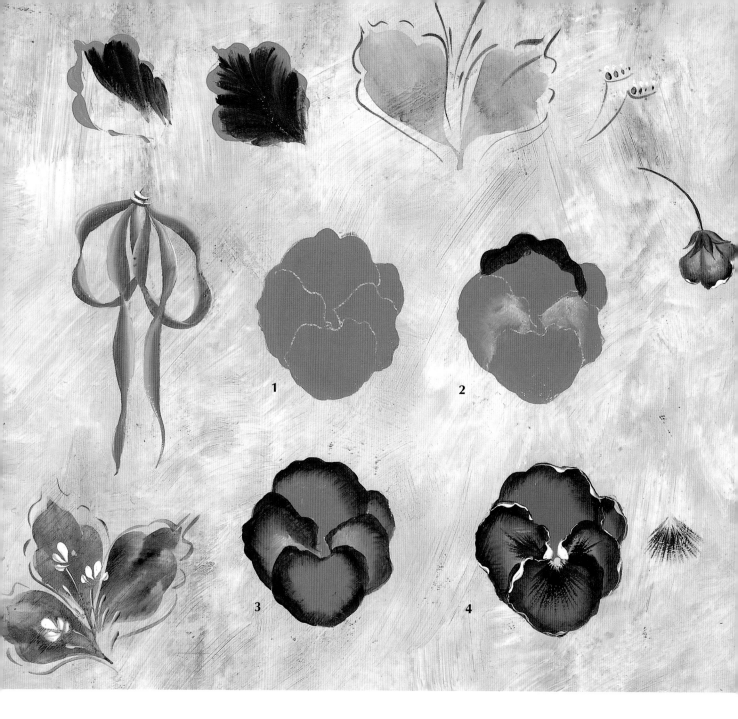

Leaves Push out the edge in Antique Gold, wipe the brush, then brush-mix Teal Green and Storm Blue and pull the Antique Gold ridge down. Don't push out the ridge underneath a pansy outline or you will end up with bumps in your pansies. Keep an eye on the direction of your strokes when you pull the ridge down as this is what gives the leaves movement.

Wash leaves Mix Storm Blue, Teal Green and some water on a separate part of the palette. As you are aiming for a transparent colour, not solid, add more water if the colour is too dark, add more paint if it's too light. Touch the brush to the paper towel lightly before going onto your piece, as this helps stop puddles

forming. Loosely outline each wash leaf with Storm Blue.

Pansies The pansies have been numbered on the pattern to correspond to the mixes below. Follow these step by step instructions for the pansy on the colour work-up.
1. Block in the shape. The colour used here is Moss Green + Burgundy + Warm White. Some pansies have different coloured petals so do all the blocking in first.
2. Retrace the pattern. Using Warm White wash a little patch of colour on the two middle petals. You may need to do this twice.
3. Starting at the back petal and working one petal at

a time, lay Matisse Burgundy around the edge of the petal. Wash the brush, dry it a little on some paper towel, and flatten out the hairs gently. It's a good idea to use an old sable brush for this. Lay the hairs along the edge of the burgundy so that half the flattened hairs touch the paint and the other half remain on the blocked in area. Wiggle the brush along and complete the petal. You are washing the colour around the edge of the petal. Some colours need to be recoated two or more times. Repeat this for the rest of the petals.

4. Using Diox Purple and the knife edge of the brush add tiny lines on the front and two side petals. Add flipbacks with Warm White. Place a Cadmium Yellow Mid dot in the centre with tiny Warm White lines underneath it in a half circle.

Following the step by step guidelines:

Pansy 1: Block in with Cadmium Yellow Mid. Wash around the edges with Matisse Burgundy lines on petals.

Pansy bud: Block in with a mix of Jo Sonja Burgundy + Moss Green + Warm White. Wash around the edges with Matisse Burgundy. Leaves and calyx are leaf colour.

Pansy 2: Block in with Warm White. Wash around the edges with Jo Sonja Burgundy. Diox Purple lines on petals.

Pansy 3: Block in with a mix of Sapphire + Amethyst 1:1. Wash around the four back petals with Ultra Blue Deep. Wash around the front petal with Diox Purple. Warm White lines on the petals.

Pansy 4: Block in the two back petals and the front petal with Turner's Yellow + a touch of Fawn. Add Warm White to this mix to lighten, and block in the two remaining petals. Wash around the four back petals with a mix of Cadmium Yellow Mid + Jo Sonja Burgundy. Wash around the front petal with Cadmium Yellow Mid. Matisse Burgundy lines on the petals.

Pansy 5: Block in the four back petals with Cadmium Yellow Mid and the front petals with Diox Purple + a touch of Carbon Black. Wash around the back petals in the purple mix and the front petal in Warm White. Purple mix lines on the two middle petals and Warm White lines on the front petal.

Pansy 6: This is a side-on flower. Block in with a mix of Matisse Burgundy + Ultra Blue Deep. Wash around the edges with Cadmium Yellow Mid.

Pansy 7: Block in the four back petals with a mix of Jo Sonja Burgundy + Cadmium Yellow Mid, and the front petal with Cadmium Yellow Mid. Wash around the edges of the back petals with Cadmium Yellow Mid and the front petal with the burgundy mix. Matisse Burgundy lines on the petals.

Pansy 8: Block in all the petals with Diox Purple + a touch of Carbon Black. Wash Cadmium Yellow Mid on the middle of the back petal. Wash around the edges of all petals with Warm White (you will need two or more coats). Warm White lines on the petals then Diox Purple over the top. See work-up.

Pansy 9: Block in with a mix of Jo Sonja Burgundy + Moss Green + Warm White. Wash a Warm White patch on the two middle petals and wash around the edges with Matisse Burgundy. Diox Purple lines on the petals.

Pansy 10: Block in with a mix of Sapphire + Amethyst. Wash around the edges of the two back petals and the front petal with Ultra Blue Deep. The two side petals are washed around the edges in Warm White. Diox Purple lines on the petals, then Warm White.

Pansy 11: Block in all petals with a mix of Jo Sonja Burgundy + Cadmium Yellow Mid. Wash around the back petals with Cadmium Yellow Mid, taking the colour out into the petals a little way. Dry. Wash around *all* petals with Matisse Burgundy. You should be able to see a little Cadmium Yellow Mid on the back petals. Lines on the petals are Cadmium Yellow Mid, then Matisse Burgundy.

Pansy 12: Mix Amethyst + Indian Red Oxide 2:1 and block in all the petals. Wash a patch of the amethyst mix (pansy 10) on the back petal. Wash around the edges of the front and back petals in Warm White and around the side petals in Matisse Burgundy. Lines on petals are Warm White.

Corner flowers   The pansies on the corners of the bed are the same as pansy 3. The buds are painted in the same colours as pansy 9. The stems are Storm Blue + Teal Green sideloaded with Antique Gold.

Filler flowers   Stems are Storm Blue + Teal Green with a sideload of Antique Gold. Little flowers are Warm White. Add comma strokes of leaf colour where needed.

I chose not to antique this piece but you may decide to, in which case you may like to use Burnt Umber oil paint. Varnish with your favourite varnish.

PATTERNS

NOTE: Many of the patterns have been reduced to fit on the page. Please check required enlargement before photocopying or enlarging by the grid method.

Teddy bear hospital trunk
page 23

Ice pack teddy

ACTUAL SIZE

Good bear teddy

ACTUAL SIZE

Tear drop teddy

LEADAVIS
©1994

74

ACTUAL SIZE

Pillow teddy

ACTUAL SIZE

75

Sore paw teddy

ACTUAL SIZE

Beary good bear

ACTUAL SIZE

These bonus teddy designs are not connected with the teddy bear hospital trunk project

Sleepytime teddy

Goodbye teddy

Floral clock

page 27

Top section

Bottom panel

join

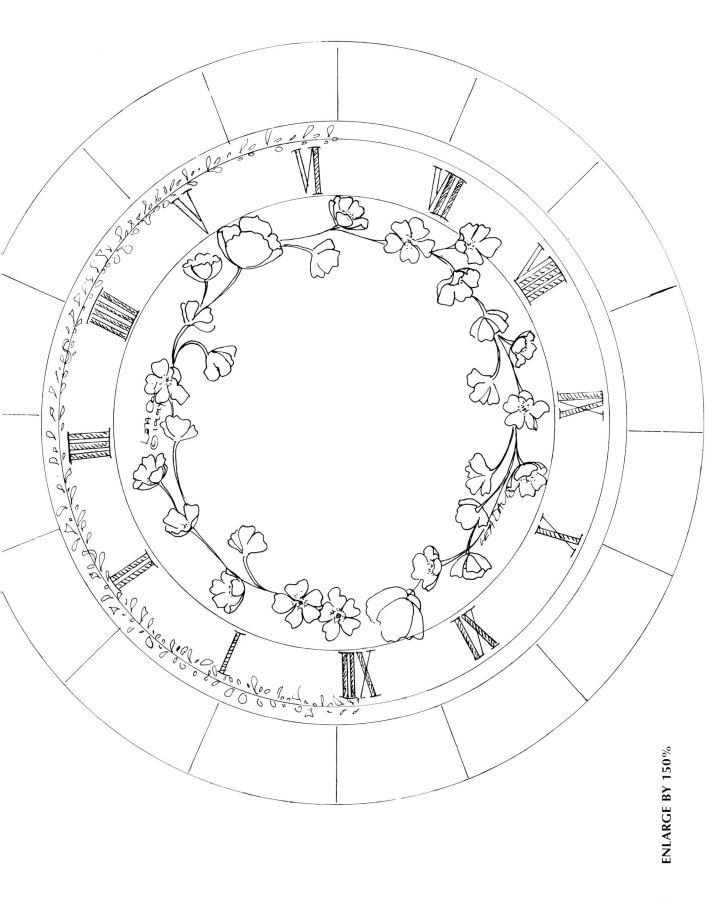

ENLARGE BY 150%

Blue stool

page 29

ACTUAL SIZE

join

join

Butler's tray

page 33

**repeat for border
around inside of tray**

*Please freehand in the wash leaves behind the design.
The pattern would have become confusing if they had
been drawn in.*

ENLARGE BY 167%

repeat for border
around outside of tray
and for the legs

85

Farmyard
cupboard
page 38

fold over
and repeat

Top door

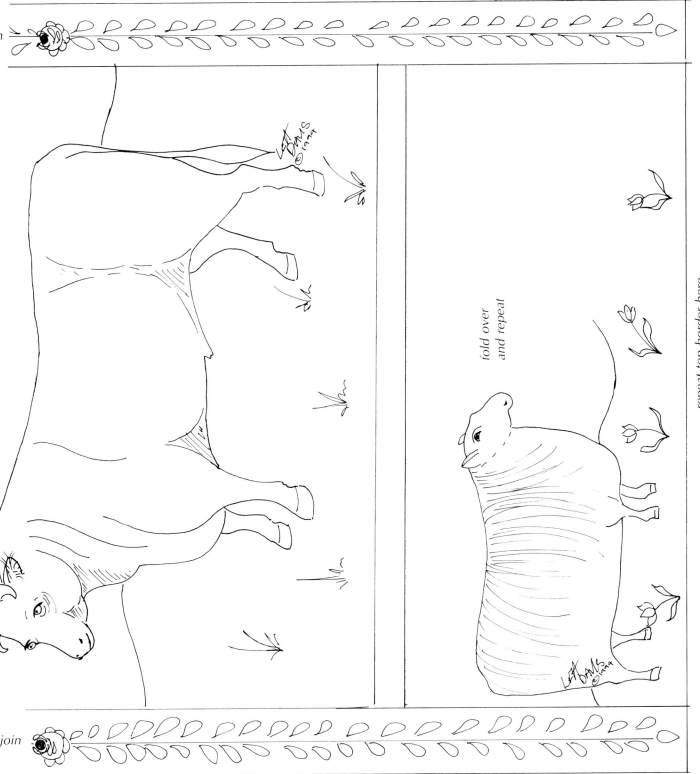

n

join

*fold over
and repeat*

repeat top border here

**ENLARGE
BY 150%**

repeat borders from top door all round

fold over
and repeat

join

join

Lower door

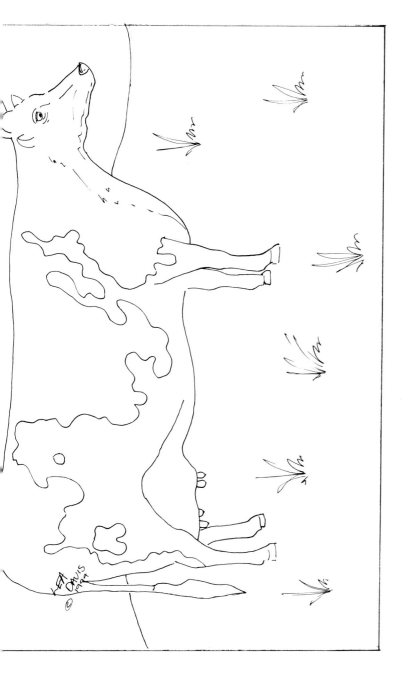

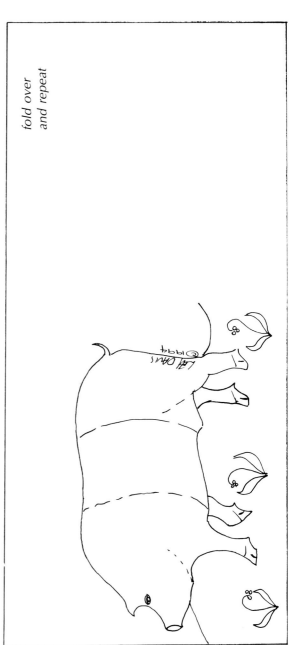

*fold over
and repeat*

Rooster cupboard

page 45

Top panel

join

ACTUAL SIZE

90

join

91

Bottom door panel
(extend sky area as required)

ACTUAL SIZE

French influence screen

page 48

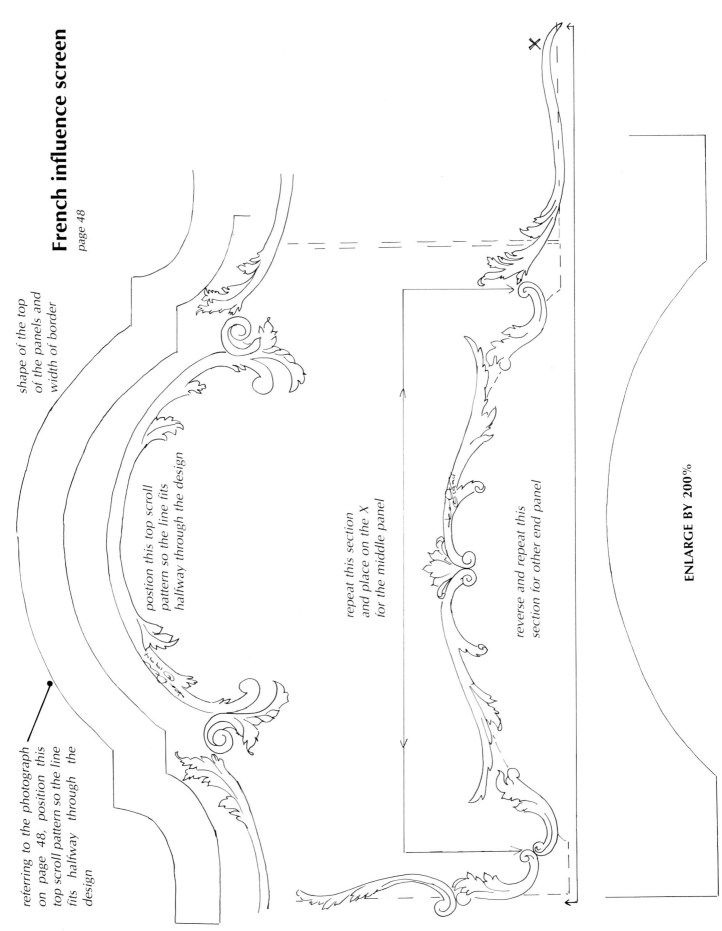

shape of the top
of the panels and
width of border

postion this top scroll
pattern so the line fits
halfway through the design

referring to the photograph
on page 48, position this
top scroll pattern so the line
fits halfway through the
design

repeat this section
and place on the X
for the middle panel

reverse and repeat this
section for other end panel

ENLARGE BY 200%

94

Middle panel

Side panels

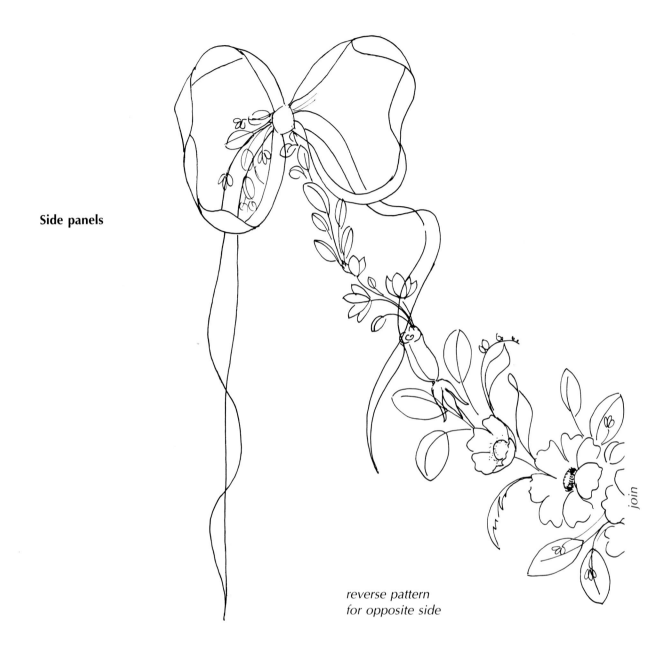

*reverse pattern
for opposite side*

join

ENLARGE BY 150%

Cherub screen
page 52

join

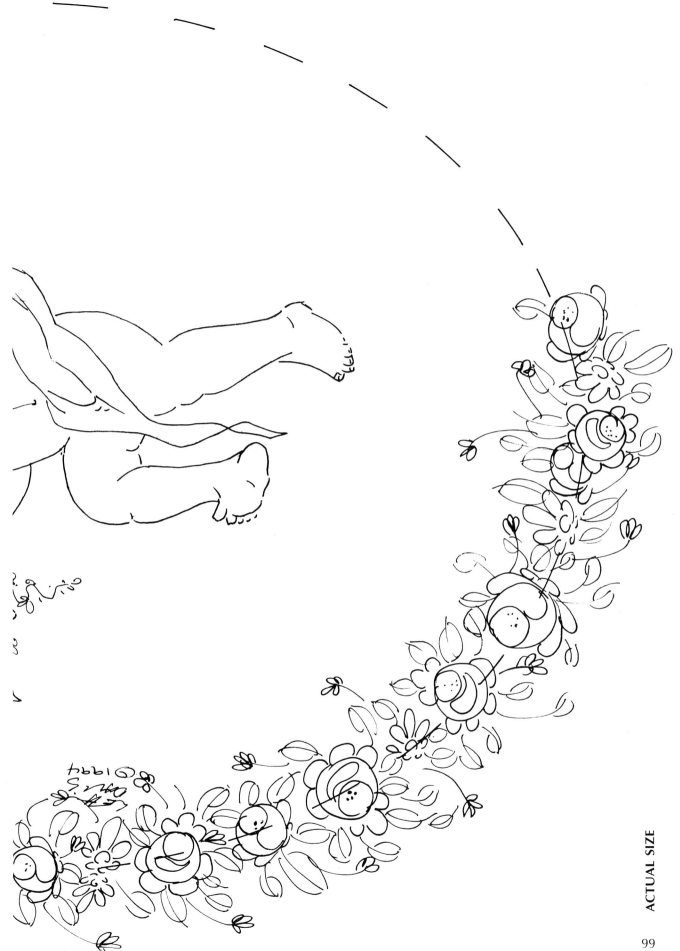

ACTUAL SIZE

ACTUAL SIZE

Schrank

page 62

Follow this guide for placement of pattern parts

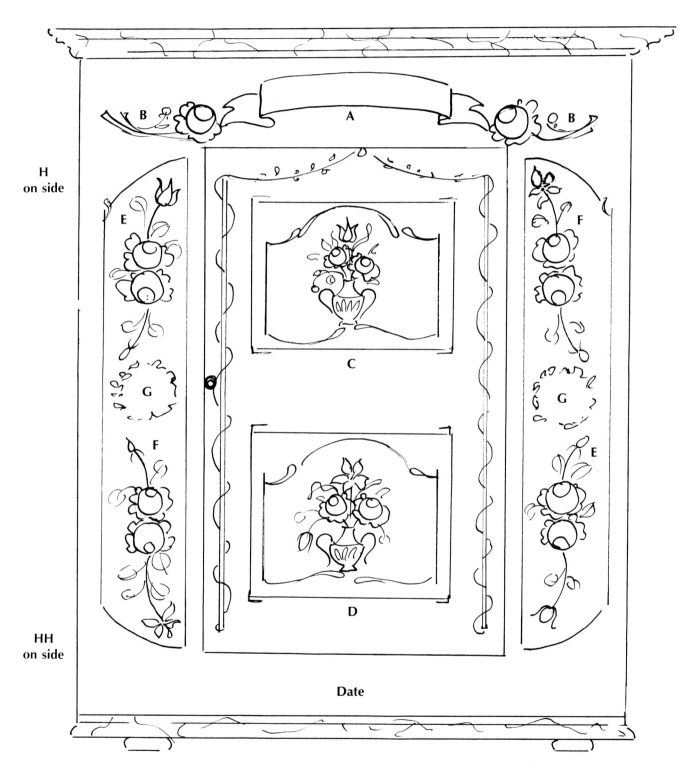

H
on side

HH
on side

NOT TO SCALE

A

Uct Justly L
Walk Humbly

G

ENLARGE BY 150%

B

D

F

Design E is placed on the top left and bottom right of the outer panels on the front of the Schrank.
Design F is placed on the top right and bottom left of the same panels

join

E

join

106

dotted lines indicate
suggested wash leaves;
add more if you feel
there are any vacant
areas

extend poles as
necessary to meet

ENLARGE BY 150%

join

H

extend poles
to required length

ENLARGE BY 150%

HH

*extend poles
to required length*

ENLARGE BY 150%

This bonus design is not connected with the projects in this book.

Topiary tree
page 58

ACTUAL SIZE

join

112

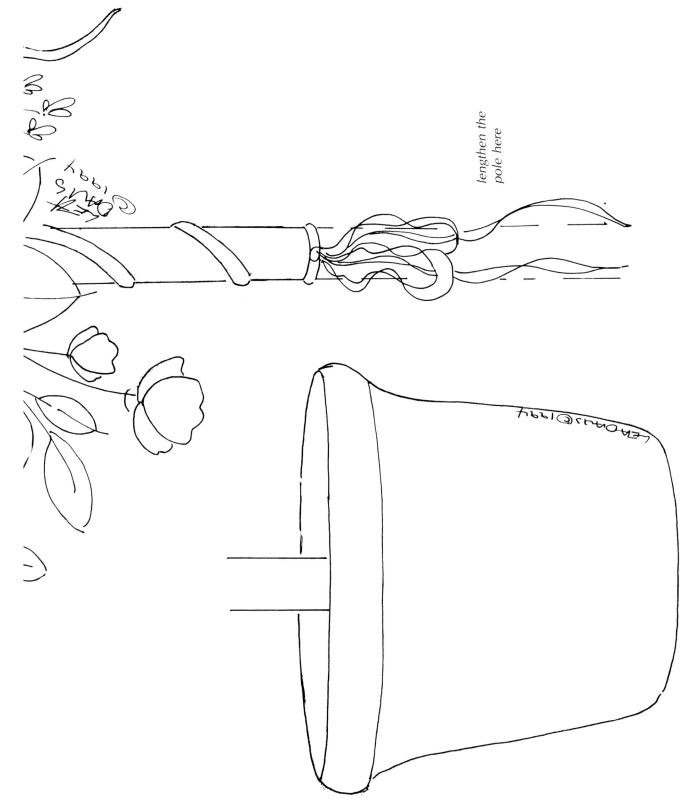

lengthen the
pole here

Pansies bedhead

page 72

W = wash leaves   *Top*

ACTUAL SIZE

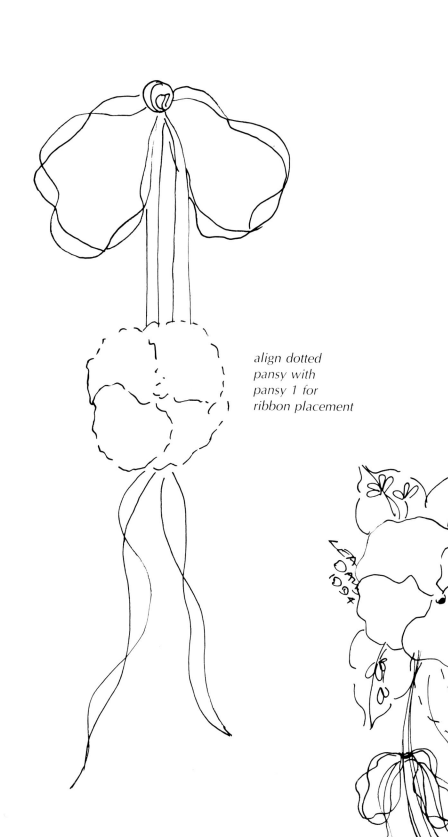

*align dotted
pansy with
pansy 1 for
ribbon placement*

ACTUAL SIZE

Corner flower

The bonus designs on these pages are not connected with the projects in this book.

Societies

If you are not already a member of the Folk Artists' Society in your state, I know you will enjoy being one.

National Capital Decorative Artists
PO Box 3018
Weston Creek ACT 2611

Decorative Folk Artists of Queensland
42 Yingelly Drive
Arana Hills Qld 4054

Folk Artists Guild of South Australia
PO Box 501
Plympton SA 5038

Folk Artists of Western Australia Inc.
PO Box 379
North Perth WA 6006

The Society of Folk and Decorative Artists of Victoria Inc.
PO Box 234
Ringwood Vic 3134

Lynne McKechnie
Folk and Decorative Artists of Australia
162 Hudson Parade
Clareville NSW 2107

Stockists

Timberturn (wholesale only)
I have included this address because Robert and Virginia have a wonderful range of wooden pieces that they are adding to all the time. Please telephone them to find your nearest retail stockist.
Timberturn
1 Shepley Avenue
Panorama SA 5041
(08) 277 5056
Fax (08) 277 5540

Butler's tray
This can be ordered through your local craft shop from:
Boyle Industries (wholesale only)
Shop 4
14 Apollo Court
Blackburn Vic 3130
(03) 894 2233
Fax (03) 894 2382

Floral clock
This can be purchased from:
Victorian Academy of Decorative Art
369 Camberwell Road
Camberwell Vic 3124
(03) 882 7082
Fax (03) 882 9128
They will be able to post this to you. Please enquire.

Schrank wood pattern
Cheque or money order for $25 please to:
Mr Frank Charlton
26 Vision Street
Chadstone Vic 3148

DJ's Colour Conversion Chart
Write to:
DJ's Colour Conversion
51 Rosella Street
Murrumbeena Vic 3163

INDEX